Reflections

in the

Dark Room

The Black Essays

Richard Kenyada

authorHOUSE®

AuthorHouse™
1663 Liberty Drive, Suite 200
Bloomington, IN 47403
www.authorhouse.com
Phone: 1-800-839-8640

First published by AuthorHouse 2/16/2009

ISBN: 978-1-4389-4799-0 (sc)

Printed in the United States of America
Bloomington, Indiana

This book is printed on acid-free paper.

In memory of
Sylvia Bullock & Edith Perry
on Herkimer Street in Brooklyn

Table of Contents

PROLOGUE   xiii

THE NEW POLITICS   1

*You should see the lines in Atlanta for early voting. And the faces of the
people waiting in lines stretching 60 to 100 minutes in length tell the story.
"This one is for Florida in 2000!"… "This one is for Fannie Lou Hamer in
1964!"… "This one is for Katrina!"*   1

We've Come a Long Way, Baby!   2
What Change Will Barack Obama Bring?   3
The Obama Effect in 2008   6
Presidential Inaugural Ball 2009   10
Michelle, M'Belle   15
The Black Vote   16
Polling the Pulse of the African American Voter   18
Election Day & Land Mines   19
The Next President   20
Jesse Jackson & The Okey-Doke   22

RACE IN AMERICA   27

*"Either we ain't black enough, or we too damn black. But I guess white folk
deal with it, too. They call it Tannin' Salons." -Barbershop Comment*   27

Black History Month   28
Black Enough for Me   30
Urban: The New Definition   31
To Protect & Serve?   32
Jews, Koreans and Arabs in the Black Community   34
On Playing "Richard"   35
Self-Portrait: In Black & White   40
One "Nigger" Away   42
Illegal Aliens, See Ya!   43

Mourning Imus in the Morning?　45
Katrina: And They Called Us Refugees　47
Letter to the Editor:Cruise Ships? Riiiight!　48
The Poverty of Spirit:Katrina and The Holidays　48
Indifference - Another White Privilege　50
Reincar-Nation　50
I'm Dreaming of a White Christmas... Party　52
Cotton: The Fabric of Our... Oppression　53
The APOLOGY, Part 2　55
The Last White Guy in the White House　59

WAKE UP! GET UP! WISE UP!　61

"Three years old, I fell off my tricycle. I started to cry and waited for my Daddy to pick me up. But he told me to stop crying, get up off the ground and pick up my tricycle. That advice worked for me then... and it works for me now." 　*61*

Black Men in Crisis?　62
Street Cred in Black America　64
To Be Young, Gifted, Black and HIV Positive　65
Gun to Our Heads　68
Black Privilege: A Sense of Entitlement to Anger　69
Internet Discussion:Black Rage & Anger　70
Battered Woman Syndrome　75
A Personal Story – The Battered Woman in the Mirror　83
Mega Church Preachers: All That Glitters...　84
Do Something!How I Became a Community Activist　85
MKN Core Values　91
Prison: Slavery, Part 2　92
Preaching to the Choir　94
"Ya-know-what-i-mean?"　96
The N Word – An Internet Discussion　97

OLD SCHOOL JOURNEY　103

"Who are we as a people that we would allow another people to put a 28-day freshness date on our history and call it progress?" 　*103*

A Change is Gonna Come   104
Remembering Sister Rosa   105
Martin was a Man   106
Frank Wills:America 's Night Watchman   108
The Next Level   110
New Year, Same Old Me   113
James Brown   115
Thanksgiving 2008   117
15 Minutes   117
Thank You, Brother John H. Johnson   119

WAR , DAP & THE BLOODS   121

*"I'm a Vietnam Veteran, and I stand shoulder to shoulder with other Vets
– the mentally ill ones, the homeless ones, the divorced and destitute, those
dying from the effects of Agent Orange, and those dying from neglect in
veteran's hospitals."*   *121*

I Am a Veteran   122

EPILOGUE   124
Wounded Soldiers: Wounded Again at Home   124
9/11 - 24/7   125
DAP: An Internet Discussion Among Black Men   127
Open Letter to George W. Bush, Lame Duck   131

BLACK LOVE   133

*"You introduced yourself, she responded with fresh conversation... She
touched your arm to make a point. ...You were free-falling from cloud to
cloud, and hoping that she would find a way to touch you again."*   *133*

Keeping the Love You Make: A Black Man's Guide   134
Keeping the Love You Make   135
The Delicate Balance   135
The Marriage License   136
Turf Wars and Boundaries   136
Two Individuals vs. The Couple   137

Another Woman   138
The Pressure Cooker   138
Commitment   139
Ajax Park   141
Love, Real and Remembered   151
Black Love: Choosing the Black Doll   153
poem for a lady loved   155

IN APPRECIATION   157

"It was at the completion of the very first senior computer workshop that a dear woman approached me to shake hands. In her hand was a tiny folded piece of paper. As she left left the library, I unfolded the piece of paper, which kept getting larger and larger. It turned out that she had given me a five dollar bill. I will never forget that moment of appreciation."   *157*

Website: If You Build It, They Will Come Mr. Kenyada's Neighborhood (1998-2008)   158

A C K N O W L E D G M E N T S   167

ABOUT THE AUTHOR   168

PROLOGUE

November 5, 2008…

When I was only 2 years old, my father taught me to memorize and recite the Preamble to the United States Constitution. I mean, I was 2, and I didn't know that many words, but I knew all the words of the Preamble. It was important to my dad, and it became important to me. He taught me to remember it in phrases, just as it was written.

We the people of the United States,
In order to form a more perfect Union,
establish Justice, ensure domestic Tranquility…

He explained to me what each phrase meant, because those are big words for a toddler. At times, I must have sounded like a cross between Elmer Fudd and a dental patient with a jaw full of novacaine. But Dad made me feel as if I were delivering the most important speech ever written. By the time I was 4, I knew the preamble backwards and forwards, and when relatives or neighbors visited our home, Dad would brag about how I could recite the historical introduction to the document that was the foundation of our nation. I would stand up on our old mushy sofa with my Dad holding my hand so I would not fall, and I would recite the Preamble like I'd been doing it all of my life (instead of half my life).

Through the years, my father remained steadfast in his patriotism. In 1963, he was the only one in our family to attend the March on Washington. Eleven years later, he passed away without ever seeing – in Dr. King's words - this nation "rise up and live out the true meaning of its creed." That's why, as I watched election night results, I thought of my late father. He would have been so proud of all the African Americans who had registered and voted. This was the big payoff that our fathers and mothers dreamed about. For decades, the voting percentages of blacks had been lower than expected, and now it was time to take our rightful place beside all other Americans in working to make the country stronger.

Yesterday, Barack Hussein Obama was elected President of the United States of America. I don't believe you heard me… The new President of the United States is an African American man. Bill Clinton can now pack away his sunglasses and saxophone. We have a real black president now.

President-elect Obama faces this new challenge seemingly with one hand tied behind his back. But he began his presidential campaign handcuffed, tied up in a sack and folded up in a locked trunk, by comparison to any other candidate. No worries. The most important thing he will do won't even make the nightly news. When he takes a seat in his Oval Office – without saying one word – he will set the bar higher for achievement than it's ever been in communities across our nation.

I know something about that kind of presidential leadership, and all that a president can mean to a kid - especially a kid made to feel invisible by society. I emerged from an era when African Americans were treated as non-entities; essentially, the Hollywood backdrop screen in the lives of white people. I was 14 years old in 1961, a year that more or less pre-dated the visibility of blacks in everyday life. Every greeting card, for every holiday, depicted whites only. The history books did not include our story. The movies rarely featured blacks and, even then, only as servants in the background. Every store mannequin was white. Every statue in the park was white. Every TV commercial; every magazine image was about white people. If you were black child, anonymity was one of those things you inherited from your parents, and their parents before them. My friends and I lived with this as our reality. So it's not difficult for me to look back and pinpoint the precise moment when I knew for sure that I was not invisible.

It was a sunny afternoon in 1961. As we played basketball at Ajax Park in Jamaica Queens, NY, my friends and I suddenly noticed that there were no cars on the Van Wyck Expressway, a usually busy Interstate that connected the then Idewild Airport to Manhattan. We kept playing, but our focus remained on the highway. Suddenly we saw one motorcycle cop, then another. We ran across the access road, and across thirty yards of grass to the edge of the Van Wyck. Then there were large black limousines, and all of us wondered what it was all about.

Riding in one of the limousines was President John F. Kennedy. His limo had a bulletproof bubble top, and the bright sun seemed to illuminate him as something larger than life. As he passed us, his car decelerated in cinema slow motion. He leaned forward and smiled that famous JFK smile. We had only seen him on our black & white TV screens, and we looked at each other, then back at him, hardly believing our eyes. As he raised his hand to wave at us, we were beside ourselves with excitement - jumping up and down, and waving to the President. The significance of the President of the United States waving to half-a-dozen "invisible" black kids cannot be overstated. No one could ever, or will ever, take that moment away from us. Finally, I felt like one of the people in "We the People..."

When I look back on that day, I see it as the day I was born, politically speaking. And that re-birth is probably the definitive affirmation an African American male needed in order to advance beyond America's predetermined boundaries. President Kennedy looked at me. And that one glance compelled me to see myself differently, and to carry myself differently from that day forward.

At some point last night – perhaps when Obama's projected tally hit 333 - I got out of bed and stood there, watching the mass of humanity that filled Grant Park in Chicago. I felt compelled to stand; perhaps for all of those, including my Dad, who could not. I had seen the long voting lines for the preceding three weeks, but it wasn't until I saw the Obama supporters in Grant Park that I finally made the connection. Closing my eyes, I felt my father's hand holding me steady on that old 1950 sofa, and his voice whispering in my ear each phrase so that I would understand: *We the People of the United States, in Order to form a more perfect Union, establish Justice, ensure domestic Tranquility, provide for the common defense, promote the general Welfare, and secure the Blessings of Liberty to ourselves and our Posterity, do ordain and establish this Constitution for the United States of America.*

I was sleepy but I couldn't sleep; tired but I could not sit down. All of the people; all of us together, with the election of Barack Obama, have taken the first step in establishing "a more perfect union." I know now, without any doubt, that I am one of The People. One other event occurred in back in 1961 that would change my life years later.

Barack Obama was born.

THE NEW POLITICS

You should see the lines in Atlanta for early voting. And the faces of the people waiting in lines stretching 60 to 100 minutes in length tell the story. "This one is for Florida in 2000!"… "This one is for Fannie Lou Hamer in 1964!"… "This one is for Katrina! KATRINA!"

We've Come a Long Way, Baby!

June 2008... If someone had told us back in 1965 – the year I graduated high school - that there would be a black president in 2008, many of us would have sworn we were watching an episode of Star Trek. After all, Star Trek is where we saw what life could be with all humans working together as equals. The right-wing would have insisted it was a fantasy, but the ground work was being paved even during the early stages of the civil rights movement.

Actress Nichelle Nichols, who played Lt. Uhura on Star Trek, once considered quitting the show during its first season because her role was so small (sitting at the console hailing frequencies). At a civil rights protest, she met Martin Luther King, Jr., who was a big fan of the show. When she told him she wanted to quit, he was shocked. "Don't you know you have the first non-stereotypical role in television?" she recalls King saying. "For the first time the world will see us as we should be seen -- people of quality in the future. You created a role with dignity and beauty and grace and intelligence. You're not just a role model for our children, but for the first time, people who don't look like us see us as equals." Now mindful of the difference she was making, she stayed on the show. Television was always at the forefront of The Movement. From the news coverage of the dogs and fire hoses in the 1960's, to the depiction of a black president in the hit series "24," TV has led the way. And now beaming across the digital airwaves is the image of Barack Obama. When his wife, Michelle, says that this is the first time as an adult that she is proud of her country, I know exactly where she's coming from. Never before has a black candidate emerged who wasn't considered a fringe element. I think it even surprised the liberals. They thought they were getting another Jesse Jackson- a rousing speech, a short surge... and then back to obscurity. And that's not meant to take anything away from Jesse. Obama knows that if Jackson didn't run in 1984, he doesn't win in 2008. If Shirley Chisholm doesn't run in 1972, Jesse doesn't run in 1984. There is a connective tissue in historical black politics, just as there is in anything else.

This is a new day, and I'm not sure it happens without a George W. Bush to precede it. This country had to see how bad it could get under the oppression of all out, unbridled corporate greed. The American people were forced to take a good, long look at itself through the eyes

of the rest of the world. We had to see the disgust in the world's eyes..
The Ugly American was just another title before the Bush thugs made
it plural. And now that they have wrung the last bit of capital from the
economy, they leave Washington's ghost town morally and financially
bankrupt.

Truly, we have come a long way, baby...

...and we have a long way to go.

June 2008 Internet Discussion: What Change Will Barack Obama Bring?

TJazz: "OK, we're here!!! The first African American candidate
for president of the United States of America - head of the highest
office in the 'Free World'. Those before us have worked so hard that
we may witness this milestone in our lifetime. They withstood bricks,
lynchings, house and church burning, rape, beatings, and, of course,
the list goes on.

So it is a given that whether or not Obama actually becomes our
next president, we're one more rung up on a ladder tilted toward an
even playing field of justice and equality. Personally, I think racism will
continue to be ongoing but this is definitely a milestone and will mark
a very significant achievement for ALL of the African Diaspora across
the world.

Yes, this is our time - our inheritance. A voice in the back of my
mind seems to keep saying, 'So, we can't mess it up.'

With all that said, and for those who have been watching the
debates and issues, what are the most pressing issues for you and what
are you looking forward to, in terms of change for us and America
moving forward?

Uhh, yes, I chose my words carefully - 'Us and America.' Feel free to
communicate your responses on one or both aforementioned items.

I'm personally not looking so much at the issues, *per se*, rather, I'm
focusing more on the methods used in addressing whatever issues are
being presented.

For example, Hillary wanted to "get everybody on-board" the
Universal Health care plan by using automatic deductions from our

wages. Here we are looking at recession in the face, and she wants to propose a remedy that assumes we can afford what we don't have. Obama, on the other hand, also wants to have his version of Universal Health care but not without addressing the costs of the same. To me, the primary issue with health care IS COST, not lack of participation."

Kenyada: "For me, the root of your question lies at the threshold of 'Change.' What will change?

The biggest change coming will be in advocacy from the Oval Office. The new president will be an advocate of the people, versus the corporation. The Bush/Cheney gang allowed corporate greed to run rampant, in every way imaginable. There was no longer even a pretense of guardianship for the American people. It was all about the corporation. Even that grand old bastard Ronald Reagan operated under the guise of the so-called Trickle Down Theory, wherein the profit of the corporations would somehow work its way down to the lowest tiers of American life. Bush/Cheney, however, even managed to shut down the damn trickle.

President Obama will, first and foremost, restore honor and leadership to the Presidency. He will not be a hand puppet for failed foreign policy, and will re-establish relations with foreign leaders in the role of partner rather than demagogue.

President Obama will be the champion of the American principle, even if he has to author the first chapter himself. And even though the challenges he faces are many, he will set out an 8-year plan to turn this Motherfucker around. He will need our help at every level of government. We must see to it that our local leaders are held accountable, too.

As for the "us" in your question... things won't change for black people until WE change them. No President can change the direction of black folk until we take the first step. President Obama (and I love the sound of that) President Obama will do what needs to be done to remove many of the obstacles and hurdles that confront us in our everyday lives, but we must prepare ourselves to run the damn race. We fought and died for a level playing field, free of man-made barriers. But as those barriers come down, we must find a way to navigate that level playing field.

Education, economic incentives, healthcare, family planning... they are all areas that need to be seriously explored. We also need jobs across this country. I'm hoping that we can institute a national project that will put people back to work rebuilding this country. I'd like to see a pipeline built as a network to carry water, not gas, throughout the country. Water - from flooded regions to regions of drought.

President Obama will not be a black president; he will be THE president, and his responsibility will be to the American people. And the best we can hope for is that perhaps for the first time, African Americans will be counted in the mix."

TJazz: "My sentiments exactly! The reason I used the health care issue as an example was to illustrate how blatantly Hillary fashions her "Mental Block" when it comes to special interests. With all of her supposed experience and political skill, she would dance around the unaccounted for high cost of health care and shove these ever increasing windfalls down the throats of the people who need it!

Obama and his disconnectedness from these special interests represent the biggest change and highest asset to his being in office. So let's just be blunt:

1. Can't tell me the war isn't putting BIG MONEY in the pockets of contractors and shareholders of those businesses involved in it - supplies, services, etc.

2. Can't tell me the skyrocketing oil prices aren't putting BIG MONEY in the pockets of OPEC leaders, G. W. BUSH, al Qaida and all the unknown interests connected with THAT farce of political and fiscal greed.

3. Good point about the water pipeline across America, Kenyada. But let's not forget the million-times-already-paid-over oil pipelines that could go in the ground and into huge resovoirs of oil in the Arctic Shelf, Alaska (yep, untapped) as well as offshore from American coast-lines.

4. Nobody in the Bush administration really even wants to fully address the jobs issues. You're right about that trickle Kenyada. That trickle was one of America's main arteries. Back then we were ripe with big corporate employers who hired American workers. Now, even a war doesn't create a job unless you're over there in it.

I think that moving forward (done right) will start out slow but will take root by the end of Obama's first term. And yes, if successful (no doubt in my mind), my bet is that he'll be there for another one."

The Obama Effect in 2008

Can you hear it?   Silence...

That's right, silence. Right there in the middle of the halls of power, where, if an old senator farts, you can hear the echo for 20 minutes. It appears that someone has posed a question that The Powers That Be are not prepared to answer. What can we do about Obama?

They don't know what to make of the Obama Effect. They didn't create it and they can't control it. They have tried everything, to no avail. The push is on to get onboard so that they can steer it away from the White House. The Liberals, too, are victims of their own bullshit this time, because they had thought that Obama was merely the second coming of Jesse Jackson. They thought they would cheer him on for the first few primaries and then he would peter out and fall in behind Hillary. Bill Clinton as much as admitted it after Obama won the South Carolina Primary, when he snidely proclaimed, "Jesse jackson won the South Carolina Primary in 1988..." They came to see a performance, not a winner. They came to see the inevitable comedy - a tap dance - not a serious drama. If they thought of this Democratic presidential campaign as a short TV skit, Barack Obama is showing them ROOTS. If the white political power structure is confused, imagine how upset and betrayed the average white conservative is feeling right about now. He wants to communicate with normal people, but he's forgotten how after eight years of Bush Bullshit – the fear mongering, the blind patriotism, the lies. He wants to find out what's behind Obama's unbridled success so that he can infuse the McCain campaign with some of it. It will never ever occur to him that it's not only about what Obama is, it's about what he is not – an old white guy plagued by wet dreams of world domination.

And the "good" white folks are left standing in the middle, borrowing the only thing Rodney King ever offered: "Can't we all get along?"

Have you noticed that whites are now more willing to engage you in conversation - not only political discussion, but discussion in general? I think it's the result of Barack Obama's success. Suddenly whites who would have nothing to do with blacks are seeking out our opinions on all things.

All their lives they have known very little about blacks – even blacks that work side-by-side with them every day. Of course, it's not entirely their fault. Thanks to the media, they have only been exposed to the Martin Luther Kings, or the Rodney Kings. But now, thanks to The Obama Effect, they have discovered the vast real estate of black folk, black thought, black deed, dwelling comfortably between those extremes… and they want in. Not necessarily to interact, but to control what they do not understand.

Republican white folks, think of it this way – y'all got Elvis, we have Obama. I think we have the edge because Obama is alive, but let's not split hairs. You believe in Elvis. You supported him in life; you support him in death. And no one had better say an ill word about The King. I get it, because that's the way I feel about Obama. He's my candidate, and he will remain my candidate. Y'all can play Reverend Wright's sound bytes all night long, but Obama is my man. You can rhyme his name with Osama, and call him No-Boma as often as you like, but we know the difference. We're gonna ride this wave all the way to the White House. And since we're kind, we're gonna let you keep Graceland and the toilet seats with the Elvis likeness. After all, it is what it is.

In mid-August 2008, the Republicans began to feel desperate. When the Militant Black Man charges didn't pay off for them, they began to hint that Obama was too arrogant. The McCain Gang was again forced to appeal to the fear of white America. There's nothing that white folks hate more than an "arrogant" black man. Whites prefer their black men docile and tame, and they love to see a smiling black man. Makes them feel… safe, yeah, that's the word. A docile, smiling black man is non-threatening, house-broken, and easily manipulated. A white man possessing the same attributes as Obama would be considered self-assured. In fact, the Republicans probably wish they had a white Obama right about now. A white Obama would save the Republican Party from itself. But, alas, they are left with just another old white guy – not even plain vanilla, because at least vanilla has flavor. So they try to formulate a jacked up character flaw in Obama – the man's too arrogant.

And while this double standard has been applied successfully over the years, America is about to undergo a major shift in its assessment of all things black, Yes, this "uppidity, ungrateful Negro" is about to save America's ass, and regain the respect we have lost around the world due to the old white guys in the White House and foreign policies. Of course, I know we haven't seen the last flailing from the McCain crowd. Expect something major in October. They want to make some kind of accusation that the Obama Camp doesn't have time to respond to before the election. That would be from the old Nixon bag of tricks.

I'm not sure that the Republicans really understand what's going on. This is not their fathers' election. You have people voting in November who never even thought about voting before. White people always vote, but I can't say the same for blacks, historically speaking. Republicans still believe they are just one dirty trick away from victory. In other words, the handwriting is on the wall... but they are illiterate.

Republican candidate John McCain was so scared of The Obama Effect that he brought onboard more staffers from the Bush team. They knew how to play dirty, because they had done it so many times before. There's nothing more desperate that an old white guy who is sinking fast. The arms started flailing about, and reaching for anything he could find to keep from going under. The Bush people had probably told him that he was too nice, and that if he wanted to win, he needed to take off the gloves and go bare knuckle.

The Obama Effect wreaked havoc on John McCain's – for lack of a better word – strategy. Two months before the election, the McCain camp went wild. McCain selected his running mate. Some say it was a bold move, but it seemed like an even more desperate move. Governor of Alaska, Sarah Palin, an admitted hockey mom with very little experience doing anything, let alone governing. Obama's success had them running so scared that they would abandon their usual Obscure White Guy strategy, for a futile grasp at the disgruntled Hillary Clinton supporters.

So how did Barack Obama overcome? How did he take his message to the American people, and persevere through every sling and arrow that John McCain and Sarah Palin sent his way? Palin appealed to the "real America," perhaps forgetting that she was campaigning to be vice president of all America. The stale ideas and attacks of the McCain/Palin camp proved to be their undoing (along with the economy). Their hate-him-because-he's-different idea soured in the throat of most Americans, making us gag.

In Looney Tunes, Wile E. Coyote always falls off the cliff, hits the ground, and gradually begins to crack. When all the hairline cracks are complete, Mr. Coyote breaks apart, and Road Runner speeds off into the sunset, "beep, beeping." John McCain's presidential aspirations began to crack long before he actually fell off the cliff. From the very beginning, he was outclassed, out smarted and ill prepared to challenge Mr. Obama.

Change. With one word, Barack Obama tapped into the wish list of ordinary hardworking Americans, as well as their college aged children, who had seen mom and dad struggle through eight years of Bush economics. John McCain, however, did not have a clue. On a Monday morning in mid-September 2008, McCain said "the fundamentals of the economy are strong." Even a healthy dose of party line Kool-Aid couldn't wash that down. And the very next day, he called the economic situation "a total crisis" and denounced "greed" on Wall Street and in Washington. It was at that precise moment of bad judgment and blind inconsistency that John McCain fell off the cliff. And if that wasn't bad enough, McCain added major gravity to the mix when he removed the muzzle from Sarah Palin, and allowed her to pass on the option of playing devil's advocate, and simply morph into The Devil.

C'mon, give me a break. Even Hillary's supporters would have to see this as an insult to Hillary and all women that the Republicans could attempt to pass off Sarah Palin as a legitimate contender. The only thing they had in common was that they both pee sitting down –and I'm still not convinced about Hillary.

The picture of the Republican ticket looked even more pathetic than it did only a few short days earlier. McCain, had just turned 72, alongside of 44-year-old Sarah Palin, who looked like Dad has just given her the car keys for the first time. If they win the election, she would be a shaky heartbeat away from the Presidency of the United States. I have a theory about Vice Presidential candidates. Weak

Presidential candidates choose even weaker running mates for VP to make themselves look stronger by comparison. George Bush (the first one) chose Dan Quayle, an unknown loser. But even Quayle couldn't make Daddy Bush look presidential. In 2008, John McCain chose Sarah Palin, who could make Dan Quayle look like a great choice.

The media is having a field day with this. If McCain wins, the world will punk us out, and even Osama bin Laden will come out of hiding long enough to drop his pants and moon the White House. To his credit Barack Obama chose to take the high ground. He knew that an early attack mode would hurt more than help. And he had the money to stay on message. The Obama Effect changed American politics because it wasn't pulled off in a smoky back room in Washington. It was planned and executed in the light of day, for all to see.

In some ways, The Obama Effect even negated White Privilege by making white folks think about their whiteness while they watch the evening news. They have never had to do that before. But now, the man who would hold the highest office in the land would be a black man, and little white kids would have to stumble over a glitch of doubt as to their chances of one day becoming president. And that's all right for a change, because for centuries black kids had to stumble into the Grand Canyon of doubt for that realization.

This is just the beginning. When Obama wins in November you can expect a new world order, a reversal of white flight, and more dinner invitations to Chuck's house.

Presidential Inaugural Ball 2009

I don't know. Maybe it was one too many re-runs of The Twilight Zone; maybe it was one too many political websites. All I know is that one night I found myself in a huge ballroom, somewhere in the middle of Washington, D.C.

Guests began arriving early. There are no place cards and no name tags. Everyone knows everyone else here. Now, there's a grand foursome - Malcolm X and Betty Shabazz sharing laughs with Martin and Coretta Scott King. Looks like Hosea Williams refused the limo again, keeping it real. And my goodness; is that Rosa Parks out there on the dance floor with A. Phillip Randolph? Geoffrey Cambridge took one look at the trio of Zora Neale Hurston, Ralph Ellison and James Baldwin, and jokingly asked, "My God, who invited my personal library?"

Seated at a nearby table, Frederick Douglass has a captive audience in W.E.B. DuBose and Fannie Lou Hamer, and Medgar Evers has just joined them. Marian Anderson was asked to sing tonight, but she only agreed to do it if Bessie Smith and Mahalia Jackson shared the stage, and they were accompanied by Marvin Gaye, John Lennon and Jimi Hendrix. Look, there's Harriet Tubman. No one knows how she arrived, but there she is. And my guess is that, when the time comes, no one will see her leave.

There's Jackie Robinson swiftly making his way through the hall as the crowd parts like the Red Sea to the unmistakable sound of applause. "Run, Jackie, run!" Along the way he is embraced by Jessie Owens. Three beautiful young women arrive with their escorts – Schwerner, Goodman and Chaney. Ms. Viola Liuzzo flew in from Michigan, exclaiming, "I could not miss this."

Richard Pryor promised to be on his best behavior. "But I can't make any guarantees for Redd Foxx and Moms Mabley," he chuckled. Joe Louis just faked a quick jab to the chin of Jack Johnson, who smiled broadly while slipping it. We saw Billy Eckstine and Nat King Cole greet Luther Van Dross. James Brown and Josh Gibson stopped at Walter Payton's table to say hello. Althea Gibson said, "You always were a charmer," as she gave Arthur Ashe a hug. August Wilson, Douglas Turner Ward and Lorraine Hansberry have just arrived from New York.

I witnessed one touching moment after another... Young Emmett Till tapped James Farmer on the shoulder. "Mr. Farmer I really don't want to sit at the children's table. We feel we're old enough to be out here with everyone else. My friends here are Addie Mae Collins, 14, Denise McNair, 11, Carole Robertson, 14 and Cynthia Wesley, 14. They just came in from a church in Birmingham. None of us wanted to miss this night." Then, all decked out in stylish evening wear, a small group of guests from the New Orleans Superdome proudly took their seats to rousing applause. It warmed my heart to see Mama Africa, Miriam Makeba, still singing and dancing pata pata style. I caught a glimpse of Lincoln Perry. He was steppin' all right, but this time he was in white tie and tails.

San Francisco City Supervisor Harvey Milk discusses organizing strategies with activist Cesar Chavez. The 60-Minutes man, Ed Bradley, just introduced himself to Josephine Baker, who flew in from Paris. It made me smile to notice how uncomfortable rodeo cowboy Bill Pickett looks in a tuxedo. Then there are the African warrior and his pregnant wife. No one knows for sure, but John Henrik Clarke thinks they could be the first Africans to have thrown themselves over the rail of a slave ship rather than take their chances with Affirmative Action. I felt a sudden chill when I saw Dred Scott speaking with Johnnie Cochran, who believes he could have won the case. Satchel Paige made his way through the crowd to greet Ossie Davis, who was sharing thoughts with Langston Hughes over there near the crystal stair. Burt Lancaster and Marlon Brando were intently listening to Nina Simone make a point, while John and Bobby Kennedy cornered Lyndon Johnson for a few laughs. All was forgiven.

Oscar Peterson is moving to take his turn on the bandstand, followed by Ray Brown. And it looks like Art Blakey and Max Roach will be keeping it tight. I spotted Congressman Adam Clayton Powell having a lively political discussion with Eldredge Cleaver, and there's Supreme Court Justice Thurgood Marshall looking on with interest. World War II Pearl Harbor hero Dorey Miller shared a few thoughts with Crispus Attucks, a hero of the Revolutionary War. And there is Madam C.J. Walker talking with Marcus Garvey about exporting goods to Africa. Look out, America - a King of Comedy, Bernie Mac, is in the house. But tonight, he is the perfect gentleman, with Lady Day and Ella on each arm. A party wouldn't be a party without the lively bunch from Galveston Texas that brought all the jubilation of their annual Juneteenth gathering.

General Benjamin O. Davis flew into Washington safely with an escort from the 99th Fighter Squadron - better known as The Tuskegee Airmen. At the table on the left are three formidable women - Shirley Chisholm, Sojourner Truth, and Barbara Jordan - gathered for a little girl-talk... about world politics. No one could mistake the men of the 9th and 10th Calvary. As they mingled among the celebrities, The Buffalo Soldiers found adoring fans of their own. One soldier looked up and told his buddies, "Sharpen up, the 54th is in the house!" noting the fresh uniforms of the 54th Massachusetts Volunteer Infantry that fought so *Glory*-ously in the Civil War.

As usual, all the science nerds seem to have gathered off in a corner, talking shop. There's Granville T. Woods and Lewis Latimer needling each other about whose inventions are better. Someone jokingly asked Benjamin Banneker if he had needed directions to Washington. And George Washington Carver was overheard asking, "What, no peanuts?" James Weldon Johnson busted out laughing as he remembered how he wrote "Lift Every Voice and Sing" as a poem to introduce Booker T. Washington at a celebration for Abe Lincoln. "Looks like I'll have to write another verse for Barack." President Lincoln smiled and nodded in agreement while refusing an offered chair. "Learned my lesson; when you sit down in Washington, they make a monument of you," he joked. U.S. Cabinet secretaries Ron Brown and Patricia Harris are heard discussing possible Cabinet appointments in the new administration.

Dueling bands? Anytime Duke Ellington and Count Basie get together, you know the place will be jumping. Tonight is special, of course, so we have Miles, Dizzy, and Satchmo sitting in on trumpet, with Coltrane, Cannonball, and Bird on sax. Everyone's attention is directed to the dance floor where Bill "Bojangles" Robinson is tap dancing. Right beside him is Sammy Davis Jr., doing his Bojangles routine. And behind his back, Gregory Hines is imitating them both. Applause and laughter abound!

The Hollywood contingent has just arrived from the Coast. Led by filmmaker Oscar Micheau, Paul Robeson, Canada Lee, and Hattie McDaniel, they find their way to their tables. At a nearby table, Beah Richards and Butterfly McQueen are enjoying a conversation with Eleanor Roosevelt and Gordon Parks. Dorothy Dandridge, looking exquisite in gold lamé, is seen signaling to her husband, Harold Nicholas, who is standing on the floor with brother Fayard watching Gregory Hines dance. "Hold me back," quips Harold, "before I show that youngster how it's done." Much laughter!

You can't miss the big smile on the face of Sam Cooke as he moves through the crowd reminding everyone that he was the first to tell us that a Change was gonna come. Meanwhile, Ellington seats Ray Charles at the piano, and Brother Ray rips into a rousing version of "America the Beautiful." My heart felt like it would burst right through my chest. I had to remind myself to keep breathing. Then a sudden hush comes over the room. A single silhouetted figure stands at center stage, and as the lights slowly come up, the crowd recognizes the man of the hour, President Barack Obama.

The applause and cheers were deafening. The President looked out across the enormous ballroom at all the historic faces. There were many smiles; precious few dry eyes. Someone shouted out, "You did it! You did it!" And Obama replied, "No sir, you did it; you all – each and every one of you – did it. Your guidance and encouragement; your hard work and perseverance..." Obama paused, catching a glimpse of his mother, grandfather and his beloved grandmother, Toot. "You would not let me fail," he said, addressing them directly.

And after briefly composing himself, he continues, without cue cards or TelePrompTer. He speaks to us from his heart. "I look at your faces - your beautiful faces - and I am reminded that The White House was built by faces that looked just like yours. On October 3, 1792, the cornerstone of the White House was laid, and the foundations and main residence of the White House were built mostly by both enslaved and free African Americans and paid Europeans. In fact, most of the other construction work was performed by immigrants, many of whom had not yet become citizens. Much of the brick and plaster work was performed by Irish and Italian immigrants. The sandstone walls were built by Scottish immigrants.

So, I guess what I'm trying to say is that the White House is, ultimately, The People's House, with each President serving as its steward. Since 1792 The People have trimmed its hedges, mowed its lawn, stood guard at its gate, cooked meals in its kitchen, and scrubbed its toilet bowls. But 216 years later, The People are taking it back!"

More applause, and recorded music begins to play. Then Michelle makes her own entrance to the music of The Pretenders – "I'll Stand By You." She walks up behind Barack, kisses him and holds him tightly, as the song continues, "I'll stand by you; I'll stand by you. Won't let nobody hurt you. I'll stand by you." That's where I lost it, and tears streamed down my face.

The President smiled broadly and took her hand as the music faded. "Today, Michelle and I usher in a new era. But, while we and our family look toward the future with so much hope, we know that we must also acknowledge fully this milestone in our journey. We want to thank each and every one of you for all you have done to make this day possible. I stand here before you, humbled and in awe of your splendid accomplishments and unwavering sacrifice. I will dedicate my Presidency, in your honor, to the principles of peace, liberty and freedom. And if it ever appears that I'm forgetting that, I know I can count on you to remind me." Then he pointed to me near the stage... "Kenyada, isn't it time for you to wake up for work? Isn't it time... Isn't it time for *all of us* to wake up and get to work?"

Suddenly I awake and sit right up in bed with a knowing smile. My wife stirs and sleepily asks if I'm OK. "I've never been better," I replied, "Never better. It's gonna be a good day."

Michelle, M'Belle

July, 2008... Let me just put this out there, right from the beginning... I would vote for Michelle Obama for President. And that dude with the same last name who is running for the office had better be thankful that he's doing so well, otherwise...

Michelle Obama will be the best First Lady since... well, the best First Lady *ever. She is brilliant, charming, attractive and savvy. And, my God, how she loves that man. She is his best friend and, together, they are raising a beautiful family... a First Family that this country can support with pride.*

Can you imagine Barbara or Laura Bush dappin' the girls on "The View?" Yeah, right! Jackie Kennedy was an aloof fashion plate in the White House, but Jackie didn't become accessible until after JFK died. Nancy "Just Say No" Reagan, too, promoted the White House as an ivory tower, far beyond the reach of the common man. Pat Nixon battled with dependency on drugs and alcohol, and was kept under wraps for most of the Nixon presidency. In fact, as you peel away the history book pages of First Ladies, you won't find another on Michelle's level in every category. She is, quite simply, the best. The emergence of Michelle Obama has even had an effect on the outgoing First Lady, Laura Bush. Have you noticed how she is traveling more now and speaking her mind? Imagine that - a black woman has freed a white woman from political bondage.

Ms. Obama serves as a role model. Not just for African American women, but for all women challenged by the duality of career and motherhood. All one has to do is look at her two beautiful daughters to understand that she has lessons to teach by example.

I love Michelle Obama, and I'm so proud of her. Barack, you are a lucky man… and I know something about that kind of luck.

The Black Vote

In August, 2005, Rev. Jesse L. Jackson Sr., kicked off a two-year campaign to extend the Voting Rights Act of 1965. The significance of the date: the 40th anniversary of the signing of the Voting Rights Act by President Lyndon Johnson. Rev. Jackson and his PUSH/Rainbow Coalition led several celebrities and civil rights activists in what was called a "Keep the Vote Alive Pro-Democracy March and Rally." It took place at the Richard J. Russell Federal Building in downtown Atlanta.

You won't find any disagreement here. The extension of the reauthorization of the Voting Rights Act was important. American men and women, of every race, have fought and died for our right to vote. There were always physical barriers put in place to keep us from voting. The Poll Tax, the silly pre-registration questions like, "How many bubbles in a bar of soap?" Our children say all of that is history, but we know better. I don't, for one moment, believe that the age of electoral racism has ended. In the old days, blacks were discouraged from voting with the threat of lynching. Today, the Bush brothers have elevated that kind of intimidation, using high technology – lynching by laptop. It is a battle we must continue to fight. The forces working against us understand that keeping blacks from the polls is, ultimately, a one-trick pony. It can only be repeated as long as no one is watching. But in 2008, everyone will be watching.

Republicans appealed to the black church in 2004, and it worked. They understood that by making the last election a moral imperative, they could win a percentage of us with the smoke and mirrors of organized religion. They know that when it comes to God, we always drink the Kool-Aid. So we have to be ready next time. Next time, we must think God, but vote smart.

It is essential in a democratic society that everyone is given an opportunity to participate in the process of its development. The vote, when broken down to its core element, is the Achilles Heel of our government. One man, one vote. It doesn't get any more basic than that. There is certain poetry in the equation – a yin and a yang, an ebb and a flow.

The vote stood at the crossroads of this nation, and it is woven into the very fabric of the freedoms we hold dear. But as essential as is this vote, it can only work as a mechanism of freedom if and when we decide to use it. And that is why I won't be attending any more marches and rallies. I won't be singing any songs or walking any march routes that lead us 40 years to the rear.

I'm a fighter, and I don't want to hear anymore songs. I want to fight! We honor those who laid down their lives when we move forward – past voting rights and towards voting responsibilities. A black vote squandered is two votes lost – your vote, and the racist vote cast against your best interests.

I want our leaders to lead us beyond their own press clippings. I want our families to ensure that each member is registered to vote. I want voter registration to be followed up by voting, a revolutionary concept – 100-percent of our eligible voters must vote. Is that asking too much?

It has never been asked, or demanded, of us before by any civil rights leader. No civil rights leader has ever admonished us – expected us – to vote; not at 100-percent, they haven't. Civil rights leaders always tell us what we want to hear. The speech is always about rights, with little said about responsibilities. As a result, we have generations of youth feeling that they are owed something, and who stand ready to collect a debt rather than pay one. We are squandering the promise we made – to ourselves, and our children, but mostly to those brave souls who brought us this far. It is time that we remember voting is a right, but it is also a responsibility.

Polling the Pulse of the African American Voter

October 19, 2008... We're within three weeks of the Presidential Election, and Barack Obama is leading in the polls from 6 to 10 points, depending on the poll taker. Poll taking has never been an exact science, but it always amuses me when the pollsters attempt to predict how African Americans will vote during an important election. For example, the numbers crunchers plugged in all the results from the 2000 and 2004 presidential elections, and have determined that 95% African Americans will vote for Barack Obama. That means that they think the other 5% will either vote for John McCain, or not vote at all.

General Colin Powell, a high level Republican, has endorsed Barack Obama for President. Perhaps some of the Republican conservative black vote – what I call the lunatic fringe element - will join us now. I doubt that the pollsters predicted that turn of events, which is just another indication that this is a brand new ball game.

I suggest that the pollsters throw out all data for African American voting in the 2000 and 2004 presidential elections. This election is very different for AAs. In previous elections, the majority of us voted against Bush, but there was a wedge created by the Republicans when they appealed to the black church, and paid off black preachers. Particularly in 2004, where the pulpit of the black church became just another campaign stop for high level Republican candidates, including Bush.

In 2008, however, there is a ground swell in the black community, and silence from the mega-church leaders, lest they suffer the price of empty collection plates. In the past, we always had to choose the better of two representatives of the status quo. Change was not an option. This year the choice is as clear as a bell. You should see the lines in Atlanta for early voting. And the faces of the people waiting in lines stretching 60 to 100 minutes in length tell the story. "This one is for Florida in 2004!"... "This one is for Fannie Lou Hamer in 1964!"... "This one is for Katrina!"

Yes, we are voting against McCain, but even more importantly, for the first time, we have a candidate for whom to vote wholeheartedly. I've never seen or heard anything like this in our neighborhoods. All across the State of Georgia the racist political structure has historically herded us into "Buttermilk Bottom" isolated pockets of political powerlessness. This is the first time that we have an opportunity to rise up, join together and, in one resounding voice scream, "ENOUGH! ENOUGH!"

I'm not sure you understand, Mr. Pollster. This vote is 400 years in the making. Pollsters don't seem to take that into account. An 82-year-old black woman had to be rushed to the hospital last Sunday in New York – congestive heart failure. One of the first things she asked when the oxygen mask was removed was "Will someone please get me an absentee ballot. I don't want to miss the election." Committed? Nah, black folks are *passionate* about this one. This is not only a vote for a candidate; it is a vote for America, the America we heard about from our parents and their parents, across the generations. Freedom and Liberty sound so trite these days, but I remember those words spoken by my Dad on his way to the March on Washington. January 20th will be a dream fulfilled. And if you are expecting only a 95% response on Election Day, you are misinterpreting the sound of the drum.

Election Day & Land Mines

(November, 2006) Another November, another Election day... I just hope it won't be another missed opportunity for black people to take the reigns of power in our own communities. We squander so many chances, but none more blatant than the annual detour away from the local polling places. Among the many ways in which we render ourselves impotent in this country, not voting should be ranked right up there at the top. It's more than political suicide; it's the ultimate showing of disrespect to those who have fought and, yes, died for our right to vote.

While it is understandable, on some level, that many of us are discouraged because of the jerk currently occupying the White House, there is no excuse for political apathy in the black community. The Bush regime has stood at the national level turning back much of the progress we have made in the past 50 years. But if we don't get our heads right, the next Republican nominee is kneeling in the batter's box, ready to use the Bush formula to nullify the black vote in 2008.

Many say that black people should not vote as a block. Well, Hell's Bells, I'd settle for black people voting 100% for Condi Rice if it meant that black people were voting. I can understand – if not totally agree – with black people being politically diverse. After all, division is as American as violence and apple pie. We know that better than many. I just hope we haven't forgotten the consequences.

Division has always been the hallmark of African American self-destruction. Historically, we were divided on the auction block. We were divided on the plantation. And after freedom, we continued the divisive ways of our former slave masters – separating ourselves according to the color of our skin and our geographical location. African Americans have become rich, upper middle class, middle middle class and lower middle class. Even poverty has its hierarchy – the poor and the working poor feel head and shoulders above the permanent underclass. We have allowed ourselves to become distrusting and suspicious of those in other classes, and we are at odds with each other.

Some would argue that white folks, too, are divided by class. Maybe so, but if you ever want to see the various white classes come together, place the interests of black folks on the table. Yes, white folks have their divisions; some are Republicans, some are Democrats, Conservatives and Libertarians. Whites are divided along lines of political ideology. Black folks are divided along lines of political apathy. The difference speaks volumes about our future. One group carves out the political topography of the nation's future. The other group is destined to delicately negotiate the placement of land mines.

The Next President

(June, 2008) It was exactly 40 years ago that a Presidential candidate emerged with the hopes, dreams and aspirations of an entire generation hoisted upon his shoulders. He was young and energetic; an idealist who wasn't looking to make a deal. He said that some men dreamed of things that were and asked "Why?"... but that he dreamed of things that were not and asked, "Why Not?" We believed in him. We believed that he would carry on the fight first waged by his big brother, John F. Kennedy, five years earlier... just before he was slain.

We had just lost Martin Luther King Jr. to an assassin's bullet, and we needed Bobby Kennedy to stand up and carry the touch forward. For awhile it looked like we had a chance to effect Change in this country. The old, grey-haired white men running the country were not only losing ground… the other old, grey-haired white men who planned to replace them were also losing ground. We wanted Bobby to set things straight. He would be the one to send FBI closet homosexual J. Edger Hoover packing. He would be the one to set the South on the path to full integration. He would be the one to end the War in Vietnam and bring our troops home.

Even the Founding Fathers knew that the greatest danger to the Status Quo was a leader who united the country across all socio-political boundaries. And just like Dr. King two months earlier, Bobby Kennedy was murdered. He had taken his Presidential Primary fight to California… and that's where it ended.

Those of us who remember 1968, watch the 2008 Presidential Primaries with hopes, dreams and, yes, fear. Barack Obama has united Americans from very diverse corners of the political spectrum. His message is one of unity and peace. He angers the Dick Cheneys of this country enough to be concerned for Obama's safety. All the pieces of the next assassination puzzle could be coming together right now. Who have they selected to be the next Sirhan Sirhan? I'm not sure this country can survive another assassination like Bobby Kennedy's.

Somehow we must protect Barack Obama, and it won't be easy, because he is a man of The People and for The People. In November 2008, the American people will have an opportunity to take this country back and bring our jobs home. With one click in the voting booth, we can confine China's lead paint to China, and bring our soldiers home to defend our borders. There is a lot riding on this election, and African Americans had better be ready. The Republicans have made their moves to intimidate potential black voters with picture ID requirements and polling place shenanigans (Let's not forget Florida!). They are doing all they can to promote black voter apathy, but we should always consider the source.

For the next few months, we need to talk up The Election – both at home and at work – to other blacks. We also need to be wary of what we hear from the church pulpit. That's how Bush neutralized our vote in 2004. He sold the black preachers a bill of goods and they bought it. Tell your preacher to stick with Jesus topics and stay away from your voting booth. They, of course, won't like that, because they feel the need to control every aspect of your daily life. In that case, maybe you will need to find another place of worship, like on your knees at your bedside.

Jesse Jackson & The Okey-Doke

By now, everyone in the world has heard Jesse Jackson's on-air comments about Barack Obama, in which he threatened to cut the presidential candidate's testicles off. Jackson whispered this while still hooked up to a microphone - a live microphone. And he committed this deed while a guest on Fox News Network. Hmmmm.

On the surface, this looks like Jesse voiced a strong dislike for, and mistrust of, Barack Obama, but all things may not be as they seem. This reminds me of the street hustle known as the Three-Card Monte. Misdirection and slight-of-hand. It's the Okey-Doke. It's that head fake in basketball that sends a defender flying up in the wrong direction while the player with the ball goes around him to make the shot.

We should be familiar with the Okey-Doke. It was last executed very successfully in the Presidential Election of 2004. Remember? The Bush-Cheney campaign convinced many high-level black ministers that the election was a moral imperative. The Black Church, particularly in the South, fell for the Okey-Doke, and the black vote was divided.

But four years later, I think we have now managed to produce an Okey-Doke of our own. The Rev. Wright's comments were the opening salvo, and the good reverend played his role masterfully. When the media ran with it, he had to emphasize black militancy early on, so that Barack Obama could rail against it as divisive and counterproductive. Many whites were harboring those fears anyway, so it was a good idea to put them on the table and dismiss them. Chi-ching, more white votes.

Rev. Al Sharpton flipped his card when he remained neutral and non-committed to Obama's campaign. He recognized that Obama would need the votes of the very same people who hated him. So Sharpton made a personal sacrifice in stepping aside and refusing to jump on the Obama bandwagon. I'm sure that many undecided white voters warmed to the Obama candidacy at that point.

The last card in the three-card Monte was the trickiest, because Jesse Jackson knew that the details would be critical, and it would only work once. This man has been in public life for almost 50 years. He has been the subject of FBI surveillance for decades. And he is supposed to have forgotten that he was on microphone... on microphone at the Fox News Network, of all places?

PLEASE! Jesse Jackson played the FOX News Network like a cheap pawnshop trumpet. He used FNN to establish distance between himself and Obama so that Obama could get more of those precious white votes. This was a political rope-a-dope, with FNN as the dope. Think about it. Any other network may not have broadcast those comments. Jesse had to be absolutely sure. What better place to perform this third card flipping than the most anti-black, conservative news network in the country? This was a stroke of pure genius.

Jesse accused Obama of talking down to black people, with his Father's Day 2008 address at the predominantly black Apostolic Church of God in Chicago. But as many black folks realize, the call for parental responsibility is really nothing new. We have always promoted the concept of black men raising their children. In fact, wasn't there a personal responsibility component in the Million Man March? So why was Jesse Jackson so angry about a bell already rung? Hmmmm.

It appeared that Jesse Jackson had lost his mind. It appeared that Jesse had been exposed as an egomaniacal monster, hell-bent on sabotaging the Obama campaign. Why? Because Jesse had no offers for a seat of power at the Democratic National Convention. Media speculation surmised that Jesse's comments were more about the messenger than the message. And that Jesse held a deep-set animosity towards Obama simply because... well, he's not Jesse.

The political pundits said that he was desperate for the kind of attention he enjoyed 1984. As usual, they said it was all about Jesse, but this is the first time the façade had cracked. They said that Jesse knew exactly what he was doing – trying to recapture a bargaining chip that he no longer had. Not to worry, they said, Jesse no longer had the juice. His tired message may be welcomed by the permanent underclass, but they don't vote. Rev. Jackson had found favor in the past with his traveling social ills show, but he always preached it to a guilt-ridden all-white choir, in an all-white church. Times had changed, they said, and Jesse could no longer successfully pull off the civil rights Top 40, because the other vocalists singing that song have learned to sing it better. And how are you going to out-Sharpton, Sharpton?

If we buy the media spin we would think that this was such a sad story. Jessie Jackson, once a powerful black leader, is now the James Dean of contemporary politics – a rebel without a cause. How could he not know this? We could not figure out who was more desperate, Jesse or Republican nominee John McCain. Jesse was in a hole looking for a lifeline to reconnect with his power base. McCain, on the other hand, was pigeon holed by the Bush legacy. In his most private daydreams, McCain probably wished he was running against Jesse Jackson. Old white men have made careers running against black candidates selling the blacker-than-thou platform. It played well in barbershops, but floundered in the voting booths on Election Day.

Barack Obama had broken away from the traditional civil rights line about blaming the government for the plight of African Americans. His message was refreshing because it spoke to personal responsibility. Had old school civil rights leaders adopted and integrated those ideas forty years ago, we would be much further along in the struggle today. No one implied that we had overcome, but it was time that we recognized our complicity in perpetuating the situation in which we found ourselves. Obama's success with whites was the result of his break with traditional civil rights strategy. If he continued to stay on message, he would win in November. Period.

But staying on message would not be enough. Obama had to distance himself from the black militant mindset as well as the traditional civil rights rhetoric. And he would need help, because he could not afford to be the one to draw the line. That would have been political suicide, with regard to the black vote. The tricky part of the plan would have to be executed outside of the Obama camp. The line would have to be drawn by Wright, Sharpton and Jackson. Jeremiah Wright, Al Sharpton and Jesse Jackson saw the writing on the wall. They realized that you don't go to the White House being Wright/Sharpton/Jackson-black. They may not have conspired, but they sure as hell figured out the best way to help Obama succeed at his goal was to establish an acceptable distance between Obama and themselves. And the beauty of it is that each of them only had to be himself.

A plan like this works on several levels, but the root of it all lies in the fact that the white power structure would never believe that blacks could even conceive of such an intricate strategy. In other words, they are the victim of their own arrogance. I believe all three men fell on their swords to ensure that Obama had a clear path to the Oval Office. The master plan was pulled off so flawlessly that even The Media, with their exhaustive research resources, was left befuddled and embarrassed. Was Jesse playing with them, or was it a tragic misstep?

If Barack Obama wins the election, the true story will probably be told, and Wright, Sharpton and Jackson will be immortalized in American History as the new Three Wise Men.

RACE IN AMERICA

"Either we ain't black enough, or we too damn black. But I guess white folk deal with it, too. They call it Tannin' Salons."
-Barbershop Comment

Black History Month

There should be a special place in Hell reserved for whomever it was that made Black History, American History with an asterisk*. And right along side of that white man, there should be a place for the first black person who accepted it.

The only reason that there is a separate Black History and an exclusive American History is that white people authored the old history books. There is really only one history, and it's called Truth.

The late, great baseball player Ted Williams, who was white and also the last man to hit .400 in a season, said it best when he was inducted into the Baseball Hall of Fame. Never much for words, Williams delivered an economical 527-word speech, and devoted 64 of those words to deliver a message:

"The other day Willie Mays hit his five hundred and twenty-second home run. He has gone past me, and he's pushing, and I say to him, 'Go get 'em Willie.' Baseball gives every American boy a chance to excel. Not just to be as good as anybody else, but to be better. This is the nature of man and the name of the game. "I hope some day Satchel Paige and Josh Gibson will be voted into the Hall of Fame as symbols of the great Negro players who are not here only because they weren't given the chance."-- Ted Williams, Hall of Fame induction speech, July 25, 1966.

After his little speech, Ted Williams, always a maverick, didn't even choose to visit the Hall of Fame. But with his speech he opened its doors to some very talented black baseball players. It took Major League Baseball five more years to finally vote an initial group of black players into the Hall of Fame. But even then, they wanted to give the honored players a separate room off to the side. Can you imagine that? They wanted to put Satchel Paige and Josh Gibson down-the-hall-and-to-the-right like they played a different game – on a different planet - loosely associated to baseball.

I heard a young person ask, "With all that is happening now, is Black History Month still relevant? After all, isn't it a part of American History?" Who are we? Dammit, who are we, that we would allow someone else to define our importance, our value and our contributions to this country and to the world... and then package it with a 28-day freshness date?

We cannot allow Black History to be experienced outside of the context of American History, because they are intrinsically bound to each other. They are two lungs of a living, breathing being known as Truth. When either is omitted, for whatever reason, Truth suffers. American History, as it has been written and accepted for centuries, has been the poorer for this omission. American His-story that does not include OUR story is a lie. American History that is void of color is lifeless. Our black forefathers breathed life into the tired-before-its-time America. The Thomas Jeffersons and John Adamses, who waxed so eloquently about Freedom and Liberty in their Declaration of Independence, knew nothing about the subjects, because they had never been enslaved. If you want to know about freedom, ask a freed slave. Ask those once in bondage what Freedom is, how Freedom feels, looks and tastes.

Jefferson and the others were the true niggers of American History. Pimpin' liberty, frontin' justice... perpetratin' revolution and slipping home to the back of the slave quarters. Tell it! White folks want American History, tell it all. Straight up, with feeling. Tell it! Fear of miscegenation; the mixing of the races? Only the white man would have the gall to fear the mixing of the races after he has screwed everyone.

Black History has a direct connection to the Black Future. And if our young people are not reminded of that on a daily basis, the future looks dim – no matter who gets elected President.

Maybe we should be concerned that the notion of a Black President will lull us to sleep, to the extent that we sit back, light a candle, say a prayer... and wait to be "delivered." Of course, that train will never come. This leg of the journey we must walk on our own. We must walk for all those who marched for us in the past; for all those who gave their lives so that we could see this day.

I love my people, I LOVE my people. But we must now stand up and walk this journey on our own, like men and women born of struggle. There was a time that we would not have let the levees break upon us. We would have stood up and linked arms and fists. We would have sheltered our mothers and fathers and stood up to hold back the tide. That kind of strength is woven throughout our history, Black History. Men and women who would bend , but not break; kneel but not fall down. We must never, ever forget our history, or the Black folk who wrote it in blood, sweat and tears. What began as Black History Week is now Black History Month. And there's no doubt that at one time it was Black History MINUTE in their eyes. But pretty soon we'll take Black History Year, year after year.

They knew we would. They knew it! That's why they didn't want us to learn how to read. Once we did, they knew it would only be a matter of time before we would learn to write, and RE-write, His-tory. Because as Dr. King said, "A lie can't last forever."

Each of us must define our priorities in this life, and something so basic as self esteem and inner dignity should never be placed on a platter for others to slice and dice. Our history is who we are and what we are. Our children need a sense of that history as a anchor, so that they can find their way home no matter how high, or how far, they soar.

Black Enough for Me

Sometimes I miss the naïve young man who once stared at me in the mirror. He had so many ideas and ideals, so many solutions and alternatives. I admired him; wanted to be more like him. There was so much room in his life that he could even accept a person like me.

He was so Black when he returned from the war. He spoke to every brother on the street, bringing his fist to his heart. He spoke in revolutionary terms - not so much about guerilla warfare, as brothers helping brothers. He had dropped the American flag and picked up the Red-Black-and-Green. He spoke of organizing, education, and shutting down liquor stores and drug dealers.

He believed - truly believed - that he alone could make a difference. And if the revolution was to begin with a holler, his would be the loudest and the longest. I loved him, but I feared for his life until he repeated what James Brown had sung about preferring to die on his feet to living on his knees. It was funny how his life was shaped around mid-1960s lyrics.

He visited me last night while I listened to my itunes playlist of several versions of Marvin Gaye's Inner City Blues. We embraced and Dap'd while listening to the song. He joked about my weight and my relocation to the suburbs ...the country suburbs at that. But it was all in fun. We talked about my work in the community, and he noted that the education initiative we launched with MKN was an activist's dream. It was about Education and Technology, and it transcended the generations to reach everyone. I was somewhat embarrassed to tell him that I've decided to tone down my activism and devote my time to writing and producing. Surprisingly, he understood, agreeing that it was time for me to shift my focus. He called it leaving breadcrumbs for those who follow.

When I wondered aloud if breadcrumbs would be enough, you know, black enough. He chuckled. "White folk sure made their indoctrination complete, didn't they? They planted a seed that continues to grow in our minds," he said.

"My brother, what you managed to accomplish with your organization, at a time when everyone else was scrambling for the cash register - well, you've paid your dues, and whatever you do now... ANYTHING, is Black enough for me.

Urban: The New Definition

Don't look now, but the word "Urban" is now in vogue. Not long ago, Urban was closely followed by words like "decay" and "blight." But now there is a flow of positivity flooding the streets of used-to-be ghetto real estate like Grant Park in Atlanta. Of course, the big draw in Grant Park has always been the Atlanta Zoo and its animals. So at some point the question must have arisen, "How do we keep the animals and get rid of the black people?" Well, they must have found an answer because Grant Park has become the quintessential core of Atlanta's white rehab movement.

And now, thanks to the media's clever city desk editors, white folks act like they discovered intown living, like it was the first mapping of DNA. So there's no secret as to the origination of the new Urban. It's all about white folks moving back to the inner city. They bring with them – along with their little dogs Toto, too – a need to once again be the majority in the inner city.

The established pattern seems to be to first declare a neighborhood to be "ghetto." Federal funding had already dried up under the Bush Administration but then, under the guise of "better housing," programs were developed that effectively removed low income residents from their homes.

The HOPE VI Program was developed by the U.S. Department of Housing and Urban Development (HUD), to demolish severely dilapidated public housing. HUD awarded $395 million through almost 300 HOPE VI Demolition grants for the eradication of more than 57,000 severely distressed public housing units.

Such programs look good on paper. Urban blight is erased and low income residents are moved to better places. But the fact of the matter is that African American public housing residents did not benefit from the long awaited replacement housing. In many cases, they were forced into already overcrowded public housing elsewhere, or they were pushed into homelessness. Where do they go when there is no place to go? Even successful small, mom-and-pop stores in those neighborhoods were demolished and removed. The only group to benefit from replacement housing programs was the mostly white middle class urban pioneers, who discovered low-density, middle class developments as their ticket on the new urban wagon train.

When the poor have exhausted all hope to remain in their homes, up pops the X Gen scouts and real estate agents, with a new marketing twist and the discretionary income to make it work. Suddenly hopeless communities are reborn as upscale white communities with price tags way beyond the reach of the low income people who used to live there.

In 2005, the United States Congress passed a resolution declaring that "the Serbian policies of aggression and ethnic cleansing in Bosnia met the terms defining genocide". Maybe Congress needs to take a good look at what's going on in urban America. How can ethnic cleansing be reprehensible in Bosnia, but perfectly acceptable in Atlanta or Chicago?

To Protect & Serve?
The Murder of 92-Year-Old Kathryn Johnston

Have the police across this nation declared war on African Americans? It is no longer safe to stay in your home and mind your own business, if you're black… even if you're an old black woman. When those badge-wearing thugs kicked down the door of Ms. Kathryn Johnston, 92, grandmothers and great grandmothers all over Atlanta must have felt a collective chill.

The Pigs – all hoods are off now – the pigs lit up Ms. Johnston with six gunshots; four to her legs, one to her arm and a fatal shot to her chest. What could she have done to warrant this horrific assassination? With the final breath she took, I imagine that she felt alone, afraid and betrayed. Sadly she was not alone. Accounts of police brutality in poor black neighborhoods are popping up, as a result of this shooting. We are finding that it is not uncommon for police - armed with unsigned search warrants – to kick down doors and break windows in the process of executing drug raids.

Of course, the monsters in blue seem to be everywhere these days. In New York City, my hometown, the police opened fire on three unarmed black men outside of a Queens nightclub which was the scene for a bachelor party. Sean Bell, 23, was shot to death, and two other black men were seriously wounded in the assault that took place in the wee hours of a Saturday morning… Sean's Wedding Day. The New York Police Department fired as many as 50 rounds – one officer alone fired 31 of the 50 rounds.

So, as police from Atlanta to New York try to cover their asses with trumped up charges of suspected drug activity, the rest of us need to prepare ourselves. The roaches of unrest are beginning to appear in the midst of this desperate situation. The New Black Panther Party has commandeered the microphones in Atlanta, and Al Sharpton is busy grabbing headlines in New York. Jesse was too preoccupied with saving the soul of Michael "Kramer" Richards to decide which flight to catch – Atlanta or New York.

This is not about the superstars in City Hall, or even celebrity civil rights supposed-to-be-leaders. This is about Black People and the Police - an ugly pimple that is about to pop. At one time we thought that more black police officers and more black police chiefs, and more black mayors, legislators, and White House cabinet members would change something that is inherently and fundamentally wrong is this society. In Atlanta, we have black people in every nook & cranny of City Hall, but Death Squads operating under the guise of police are still raiding our communities - quick to the draw, armed to the teeth, and not above planting "evidence" to justify whatever they do.

We keep expecting the police credo - "To Protect & To Serve" - to apply to us. But after crossing the border into our communities, protect and serve quickly becomes harass and intimidate, and assassinate.

Wake up, wake up! The alarm is ringing!

Jews, Koreans and Arabs in the Black Community

A media firestorm has erupted in the aftermath of former Ambassador to the United Nations, and former Mayor of Atlanta, Andrew Young's comments about the motives of Jews, Koreans and Arab business people in the black community. Not only did he feel compelled to apologize, he was apparently pressured to resign from his position with Walmart. But did Andrew Young lie when he blasted Jews, Koreans and Arabs in our community? Most black folk were probably surprised by Young's comments. Not because they weren't true, but because they never thought anyone of his stature would "tell it."

The fact is that countless Jews, who are former slumlords, now reside comfortably in Florida. They made their money in the 1950s and 60s inner city ghettoes selling, as Young said, "stale bread and bad meat." And as they pulled up stakes, escaping to Miami, the Koreans moved in with their wig shops and semi-rotten vegetables. The Arab wagon train was not far behind, with their car title loan, pawn shops, and every Dairy Queen west of Philadelphia.

Do you remember the scene in Spike Lee's "Do The Right Thing?" Three black men are sitting across the street from a Korean grocery store, bemoaning the fact that Koreans jump off the boat, and immediately head toward our community to set up a business. That must be one helluva Business Plan. A grocery store is one thing, but how does a Korean demonstrate an expertise in black hair care? What kind of loan officer buys that story? And, further, would that same loan officer stamp an approval on a black man's application to open an Asian market in the middle of Korea Town? Or how about a much needed driving school in China Town? I don't think so.

Of course, Blacks must share the blame with the slumlords. They could not exist without our patronage. It's a symbiotic relationship that resembles that of the moth and the flame, the needle and the junkie. Someday we will wise up, and some unknown comedian will lay it all out on stage … didya hear the one about a Jew, a Korean and an Arab going into the black community…

And absolutely NOTHING happened?

On Playing "Richard"

No, I'm not really Richard, but I play him at work.

For over 40 years, I have played the character "Richard" in the longest running off-off-off-Broadway production in history. I have worked in the engineering profession since 1969. When I broke into engineering, at the age of 22, I didn't think I could deal with the overt/covert racism and bigotry that confronted me everyday. I was the only black person in the large engineering department. It was a mental challenge just to walk down the aisles. I walked a gauntlet of precision steel stares simply on my way to the restroom.

Practically fresh out of the military and having survived two tours of duty in Vietnam, I wasn't about to accept any racial nonsense from anyone. Neither would there be any ass-kissing or kowtowing. There were certain things that I was simply unwilling to do, and those things had nothing whatsoever to do with the job. I was new to the profession, but I was also hired to do a job that was usually filled by a white man. Some of the old white men who were already there did not hide their displeasure in my presence, and had I been another kind of black man, I may have been intimidated by their attitudes.

Everyday, I'd go home on the subway absolutely percolating with anger. I had to find a way in which to deal with those people at work that would not compromise my job… or my dignity. Dad always told me that they can take a lot from me. But they can't take your dignity, he said. You have to give them that. Never let them disrespect you.

Within the course of those first few days, I created the character of "Richard." There was no identity conflict, either, because my friends knew me as Harp, and my family called me Richie. So "Richard" worked perfectly, because it was my given name, and each time someone spoke to me at work, using that name, it reminded me to stay in character.

When requests or conversation overstepped the bounds of his character, Richard simply responded with "No," or "No thank you."

Company Christmas Party, "Richard... will you be there?" "No, I won't." "How about a drink around the corner at Happy Hour?" "No thank you." "Hey, would you like to see a photo of my dog?" "Hell No!... Thank you."

Richard quickly developed a reputation at work for being a no-nonsense guy, who did the work well, but was totally anti-social on any other level. I soon found that I could jump into, and out of, the Richard character at lunch time. That was a major discovery because it meant that I didn't have to keep up the charade non-stop throughout my entire work day. It was like being Clark Kent at work, but looking forward to the next time I could fly, when my workday ended.

After three years, I moved on to another firm located a few floors above in the same building. I applied for a Structural Drafting job during lunch, and was hired immediately after two interviews. It all lasted less than an hour. My Vietnam Veteran status had opened the door for me, and the quality of my drawings did the rest. On the first day, I met a senior draftsman. He was a black man! And after three years of working in Beaver Cleaver's house, this was a sight for sore eyes.

Willis Atwell, 45, was about six feet tall, with an almost white complexion, blue eyes, and sandy light brown hair. We quickly warmed to each other after he wondered aloud how I could have survived downstairs at the other firm for three years. We both had to laugh out loud, and after that moment, he became an older brother to me. Willis was married with two teenaged kids, and he told me about his battles at work over the years. I told him how I had dealt with my challenges at my previous job. I let him in on the development of the Richard character, and he understood the reasoning behind it. But he also told me that he'd be there to watch my back. Smiling, he told me that if he ever saw me ready to blow off steam at someone, he'd call me "Richard." We both busted out laughing again. It was then that I realized that the previous three years was just a job, but that day was the first day of my career.

In 1975, Willis became my role model, when I found out that I was going to be a father. Two months before my son was born, I petitioned the New York City Civil Court to have my last name legally changed to "Kenyada," so that my kid would not have to live with a slave sir name. I kept "Richard" because it had, by then, become a comfortable at-work identity. A funny thing happened once the name change became legal. I was able to shed much of the hatred I harbored for white people, in general. It seemed like a weight had been removed from my shoulders, and I could raise my son from a fresh slate. Willis understood, and was the first to address me by my chosen name - except at work, where I remained "Richard."

In 1978, my family and I decided to move to Atlanta, and one of the hardest things I've ever had to do was to say goodbye to my good friend Willis Atwell. A few years after that, he lost a long battle with lung cancer and died. It was, indeed, like losing my brother. I was totally devastated upon hearing the news from his wife. I could not even bring myself to attend his funeral.

Years earlier when I mentioned to my Dad that I was considering moving South, he almost begged me not to go, fearing for my safety. He told me about the Old South and the lynching. He told me about the disrespect that would await me around every corner. My Dad was an old-line fighter for integration. He joined with Dr. Martin Luther King, Jr. and about a quarter-million others in the March on Washington back in 1963. I loved my Dad and I respected him. And I know, like any Dad, he was just trying to protect me. So I reassured him that I was not moving South to integrate with white folks, and that there was no reason for him to worry about me or my family. Of course, what I didn't tell him was that I had witnessed, at a very early age, the effect white people at his job had on him. He would deal with their bigotry and condescension by day and, at night, find relief at the bottom of a Scotch bottle. Superman had his Kryptonite; my Dad had his White Horse Scotch, with much the same effect. The difference was that Superman didn't have children watching him in his weakened state. It was an education that would serve me well, in my relationships with white people at work, particularly in the South.

Everything I read told me that the South held more than just the past of African Americans; it held the Future. And while many black families (including my Dad's) had fled the South during the early 1900's, generations later, many families were coming back. But I wasn't coming south to seduce a white guy's girlfriend, or to marry an old white man's daughter. I damn sure wasn't moving South to live next door to whites. I was moving South to LIVE! Period. If that alone would target me for their hate, then bring it on, damn it, BRING IT ON.

The "Richard" character continued to develop in Atlanta. They say that Atlanta is part of the New South, but for a black man, in many respects, it's the same old shit in a different package. The racism and bigotry still exists here, but it wears a smile. They've learned how to change the costume and the script, but it's the same old plot. They prefer to see a black man in the end zone of a football field, rather than the Oval Room in the White House. If the 2008 Presidential Election taught us nothing else we learned that racial harmony is just a facade. The work atmosphere in the professional environment is not much different than it is in the blue collar environment, except maybe a little more sophisticated. They don't call you "Nigger" to your face, preferring to legislate and regulate the terminology into something resembling decency. But the results are the same. Sometimes you just want to stand up and scream out, "Damn it, just call me 'Nigger' and get it over with, for Chrissake!" But that's not Richard's style.

Up North I had to work along side suspected skinheads, Mafia and neo-Nazis, but down South there were red neck Confederates who cherished their racist heritage like it was as pure as driven snow. So it was very easy for me to distance myself from them. I didn't take any shit in New York, and I wasn't about to take any in Atlanta. But some white co-workers would not take "No" for an answer, and one decided to challenge my decline of his personal invitation to the company cookout, which amused me to no end. He wanted to know "Why?" Forget the fact that this was my personal choice, I suppose he took it as a personal challenge to bring me in line to drink the Kool-Aid on the company "family."

White guys, particularly professional-type white guys – are hilarious when they're trying to be serious with a black man. There's a whole different body language involved. They want, I swear, to be "down," but bless their little hearts – they wouldn't know "down" if it were stamped on their foreheads. They make a move towards you, because they think they need to invade your space in order to get their point across. Black people don't operate well in that up-in-your-face mode, unless we are ready to kick your ass – then, all bets are off. Anyway, the white guy gets up very close and asks me, in that whispered Dudley Do-Right voice that Richard Pryor made so popular, "Richard, is it that you don't like white people?" "You're white!?" I asked, feinting terror (In my white Dudley Do-Right voice. And, yes, we have one, too. And it will take him five hours before he realizes that I was mocking him with that voice. He'll be home playing Parcheesi with the kids and it will hit him… "You're white? I asked rhetorically, "I thought you were my co-worker, and you weren't white until you were outside of the building. You know, like I'm black outside of the building… or inside the building if you're speaking with a white friend and I pass by… whichever comes first." Poor Dudley didn't know whether to laugh or get even more serious. He decides on the Dudley chuckle, and walks away.

These people are not in my league. I am a professional black co-worker, and it ain't even a fair fight. I've done this for almost 40 years, and no one, not even Sidney Poitier, does it better. Actually, I probably do it too well, because every year someone asks me the same dumb-ass question. "Are you coming to the Christmas Party?" You would think after 20 years of working in the same firm, they would know the answer. But I have a theory about that - I really don't think they listen to the answer. It just must be something they ask me as a Christmas tradition, like watching Jimmy Stewart's "It's a Wonderful Life." Their holiday won't be complete until I've declined their invitation to dinner.

"Richard" knows how to get along with everyone, and make them all feel comfortable. First of all, they know that I don't gossip, because I don't really speak to anyone about anything that's not work related. They can trust me with their innermost thoughts. They also know that I stay away from office politics, and I don't choose sides. In short, I'm usually a pleasure to be around. "So why won't he break bread with us?" is what they probably ask each other each year. They'd never guess that the answer has more to with their "bread" being stale enough to "break" than anything else.

As civil as race relations at work have remained over the years, it wasn't until the 2008 Presidential Campaign that racial tensions were exposed once and for all. The white Republican bigots could not contain themselves any longer. The mere mention of Obama's name was cause for a political "discussion." It got to the point when management felt a need to post an article on the company bulletin board that suggested the workplace is no place for politics. I wore an Obama cap, and adorned my car with an Obama bumper sticker. I did not discuss Obama, but I made it very clear where my alliances were. Barack Obama epitomized my 40-year struggle against workplace bigotry, and I wasn't about to miss the opportunity to "exhale."

Developing the "Richard" character over the past four decades has allowed me to keep my work life and home life totally separate, ensuring that I remain efficient, productive... and sane at work. And very happy and fulfilled at home. "Richard" is my portrait of "Dorian Gray," suffering the boorish conservatives at work so that I can make a living while pursuing other goals I really care about. It's the kind of perfect balance that Willis Atwell would have understood and appreciated.

I really miss him.

Self-Portrait: In Black & White

I used to believe that no one is Black all of the time, 24/7. Even Malcolm X must have had private moments with Betty Shabazz and the children, that were just about being a family, as opposed to being a black family. I know that sometimes I just don't feel like being "black," whatever that is these days. I just feel like being. It's the kind of burden that no other race is faced with on a daily basis, and it can be very tiring, having to jump in and out of character on a moment's notice.

Recently, I drove out to East Cobb Park, which is located in a white upper middle class area, to take some photos of a pedestrian bridge we had designed and built. I had my iPod plugged into my ears and Kirk Whallum was playing The Babyface Songbook. Man, was I relaxed! It was a beautiful little park with a stream. The setting could not have been more conducive to mellowing out on an unusually warm winter day. I was just a person walking along a pathway in a park. After photographing the bridge from every angle, I walked back to the parking lot, which was just off Roswell Road.

I saw the East Cobb Park sign at the curb, and I thought it would be a nice touch to include a shot of it for my marketing sheet. Then it happened… Between my first and second shot, I heard the unmistakable sound of tires screeching. It was a Cobb County Police patrol car. Click! OK, now I'm black again… if ever so reluctantly, because part of me wants to believe that there is some sort of crime taking place in the park and he was directed to check it out. I continued taking photos of the sign and the park entrance. I then noticed that The PIG – yep, I'm all-the-way black by then – the Pig had made a u-turn in the parking lot and pointed his patrol car in my direction. He remained there – eh, coincidentally? - until I finished shooting and returned to my truck. Absolutely seething, I put my camera away, momentarily considering a shot of The Pig. But Thinking Black told me not to give The Pig an excuse to fire a warning shot through my view finder. Knowing, too, that no jury in East Cobb would convict him, I just left the park, hoping that no White Person back at the office said anything to me for the rest of the day.

It's funny, because most of us go through major portions of our day without having to carry the extra weight of Being Black. We can just be loving, or funny, even sad, or deeply engrossed in a good book, without ever thinking about race. That's the ultimate freedom. But then it happens – we see the evening news, or hear the voice of George W. Bush, or make the mistake of crossing paths with Cobb's finest. Usually for me, that's all it takes.

As my other self – Richard - I'd rather ignore them all than make allowances for a few. Indifference makes for a simpler accounting. But now and then, I run across a person who happens to be white, as opposed to a White Person. There is a difference, you know. A person who happens to be white (PWH2BW) relates to you as a person who happens to be black (PWH2BB) - a colorless, race-less mind and spirit, that is uniquely individual. Humanity is seen as a common denominator rather than an accidental freak of nature.

I find that I have more patience with PWH2BW and PWH2TBB than with white people and black people. I'm more at ease with educated PWH2TB than those who wear their race on their sleeves, forever trapped in a shoebox of racial stereotype and ignorance. I used to try to fit in on the black side, until I realized that we are all a mixture of our environment and experiences. I love kosher deli foods, but I'm not a Jew. I make a killer shrimp egg roll, but I'm not Chinese. I hate pork chops, collard greens, and sweet potatoes… but I am black. Go figure! Being black is not a robe we wear or a food we eat. It is a state of mind. Even if we disregard the color of our skin, we are still black. I've known some white people who are black, by nature of their vibe. The Black vibe is the Blues/Jazz soundtrack that is stitched throughout the fabric of our lives. That is not to discount the classical/operatic vibe that may also play in the background, but blues is at the roots.

Education makes a difference only in that it gives us a higher perspective from which to chart our direction. We need to rise above the buildings and the shadows in order to see where we need to go. The black brother hanging on the street and the brother on his way to class may both briefly share the same street corner. But the brother on his way to class sees that corner from a different perspective – a mile above it.

While being black may be a minority position, being educated and black is a smaller minority. Being educated, black and active in The Struggle, may nowadays be a much smaller percentage than Dr. Dubois's original "Talented Tenth." And I remain concerned that we have lost touch with each other, and that our historical common bond is something now more readily displayed on our coffee tables and bookshelves, than in our hearts.

One "Nigger" Away

November 17, 2006… Actor Michael Richards, who played Kramer in the 1990's smash hit series "Seinfeld," became the latest celebrity to get caught with his PC pants down. While doing a stand up routine at a Sunset Strip comedy club, he was heckled by two black men. Richards went into a rant, using the "Nigger" at least a half-dozen times. He said, "Shut up! Fifty years ago, we'd have you upside down with a fuckin' fork up your ass."

Of course, he now sees the error in his ways – they always do, don't they? The man's waning career desperately needed publicity – good or bad. Now he gets to appear on Letterman and other talk shows to apologize. It puts him back out there… for a minute.

I only mention this because once again it's that time of year when white co-workers will want to go out, have a drink, break bread together. And all across the country black folks will set themselves up to be humiliated and betrayed by people they wish to befriend. The fact is that we're all just one "nigger" away from disillusionment about our white co-workers. One fit of anger; one OJ Simpson verdict away from clarity about the race issue in America.

A female friend who prided herself on having a rainbow of friends, was working late in her cubicle one evening. Her "best friend white girl" was also working a few cubicles down. She didn't know my friend was there. A couple of white maintenance men were trying to secure something on a moving cart, and the white woman needed them to add a piece of furniture to the pile. They didn't know how they could secure it all. She advised them to "just nigger-rig it." My friend was stunned as she listened. She had never heard that term before. Stunned and afraid to let anyone know she was there, she waited until they left. She could hardly wait to tell me that I had been right. The curtain had been raised on her friendship to expose it for what it was.

My Dad once warned me to never position myself between "a white boy and a pitcher of beer." He said that I would be terribly disappointed if I sought to befriend them. His wisdom has never failed me. I have many things to pass on to my own son, but I let him find out about the race thing by himself. I didn't want to burden him with my truth... wanted him to find a truth of his own... and he did.

Michael Richards only exposed himself on that stage, not white America. He let go of the restraints and busted his racist gut for all to see and hear. People like me are generally not surprised, but perhaps we are a little disappointed, once again. And once again, I will respectfully decline the offer to see my white co-workers through the prism of a pitcher of beer. I've long ago given up on saving myself. Now I just try to save some white people from themselves.

Illegal Aliens, See Ya!

I don't know precisely when it happened, but sometime in the past ten years, a media editor changed the word "illegal" to "undocumented," and "alien" to "immigrant." And with that swift movement of the red pen, that editor contributed to the erosion of American justice. The term "illegal alien" joined the ranks of "wetback" as an offensive slur, rather than a point of fact.

In the early 1900's, when some Italians came to this country illegally, in the cargo holds of Trans-Atlantic ships, they were ostracized as WOP (Without Official Papers), even by their own people. They had broken the laws of a nation and no one sided with them.

I don't understand the problem. Millions of people have –over the years – crossed the borders of the United States without proper documentation. Now numbering approximately 12 million, they have lived in this country without applying for citizenship, yet they have reaped many of the benefits given to citizens of this country. They have lived here without serving in the military or submitting income tax returns. They have lived here sucking up medical and social services, making it more difficult for legitimate US citizens to find or afford those services.

They say that they come here seeking economic asylum, not political asylum. When the Haitians came here in droves claiming political oppression, the US government said they were really economic refugees, and returned them to Haiti. In other words, these Mexican illegals are about eight shades lighter than a U-turn at the border. At 12 million, maybe the numbers look too massive an infraction to make right. So let's use a one-on-one analogy. Let's say I have a big house – so big that I rarely use the finished basement. My neighbor has a few visiting relatives, the Mantillas, who need a place in which to stay. Instead of approaching me to ask whether I can help them by suggesting an agency or alternate living arrangements, the Mantillas decide to take what they need. They wait until my family is at work and school, and they sneak into my house through a basement window.

Months pass and the Mantillas have become quite comfortable living in my basement. After all, they use my water, gas and electricity. They keep the basement tidy just in case I happen to need something from storage. When we are away from home, they steal food from my refrigerator and pantry. [That's right, If they're here illegally, everything they take is theft] They watch my big screen TV. They have even found a few neighborhood odd jobs, the salaries from which are often sent to my next door neighbor's house. After all, they are family.

Of course, it's not all about perks. They live with the constant fear that they will be discovered and removed from my basement. But they are beginning to feel even more comfortable. The mother, Maria Mantilla, is pregnant and will have her baby while living in my basement. Already they are looking into the laws to see if a baby born in someone else's house can legitimately be counted as a member of the homeowner's family.

Undocumented immigrants who have entered the United States illegally from Mexico, Central and South Americas need to be returned to their respective countries. At every undocumented immigrant rally, there needs to be 3,000 Greyhound buses, with a little sign in the destination window that simply says, "ANY PLACE ELSE."

Illegal Mexicans think this is all about their freedom to find work here. But it's really about the leisure time of The White Woman. Beginning in the middle 20th Century, Black women began to enroll in college in record numbers. And as that generation of college educated Black Women graduated, with far more career opportunities than ever before, White women discovered that they needed homemaking help. Not that the discovery is of monumental importance. Throughout American History, white folks have survived on the labor of people of color - whether in the fields or in the kitchen. It's time that they sully their hands and work up some calluses in their own fields and laundry rooms. And I don't care if every white, well-to-do woman in America has to baby-sit her own children, wash her own laundry, pick her own apples, or wipe her own ass, for a change.

Mourning Imus in the Morning?

In the April 4, 2007 edition of MSNBC's Imus in the Morning, host Don Imus referred to the Rutgers University women's basketball team, which is comprised of eight African-American and two white players, as "nappy-headed hos." Then, a little over one year later, in June, 2008, Anus, eh, Imus, made another racially charged comment about football player "PacMan" Jones.

There is nothing quite as pathetic as a bigot who envisions himself as a liberator. Don Imus has been on the radio forever. And while his audience used to consist of the ultra hip underground, these days his appeal has dwindled to hardcore losers - white guys too busy watching the walls close in to do anything about it. Imus, one of the original shock jocks, has been reduced to the poster child for middle-aged white guys with race issues. They blame educated black women for the loss of their jobs. And it's not surprising that Imus' racist rant about the Rutgers basketball team was such a hit among his diehard audience. With his bigoted comments, he was striking a blow for every white male loser in the country. And their numbers are legion.

I work with losers like these every day. They are the college age and middle age white men who are slowly losing their identity as "Masters of the Universe." All these years, they have enjoyed a reign of superiority that afforded them First Class status, even among their own women. They are border line skinheads and "rednecks," who feel better about themselves when they degrade others, particularly black folks. They lead a pathetic existence that requires the presence of underlings - real or imagined - in every aspect of their lives. Shock jocks and conservative broadcasters feed that need with anti-minority commentary and observations.

Clearly, the Federal Communications Commission has much to consider, as do the advertisers that support such programming. But the black community doesn't get a pass on this issue. We've got to do some house cleaning, too. A few days after Imus' bigoted comment, a few rap artists denied any parallel between Imus' comments and their own lyrics about "bitches" and "ho's." The difference, in their minds, centered on the fact that Imus was talking about college women, and rappers are just referring to neighborhood women. And these are the people who have an influence on the minds of our young?

The mind-set is out there. We have disrespected ourselves to the extent that others have chimed in on cue. Am I surprised that a bargain town bigot has adopted our own anti-black racist remarks? No! Am I incensed that Imus felt comfortable enough to use such terminology on national network radio with impunity? Not really. I used up most of my anger when black people first started calling each other niggas and ho's. I was incensed way back when hardly anyone – including most young black women - found rap lyrics insulting to black women.

We have to ask ourselves how much blame we are willing to accept. We have always had to endure racists and bigots. The difference is that we have adopted their negative words and images to make them popular, and the descendants of the original racists are now using this material as a rallying point.

Mourning Imus? Not hardly. His comments are hurtful, but he is only one pimple on the ass of broadcast entertainment. I'd prefer to be mourning the demise of the black rap artists who made those comments relevant in any discussion about race relations. As we used to say back in the day, "When the revolution comes, we will have to lose some of our own."

Katrina: And They Called Us Refugees

The enormity of the damage caused by Hurricane Katrina is difficult to fully comprehend. There is the short term damage – death and destruction; the mid-term damage – evacuation and medical care. But in the long term, there is a psychological imperative that threatens to divide and cripple this country for generations to come.

Racism and Class-ism is an ugly seam in the very fabric of America. Over the past 50 years, the seam has been delicately stitched, patched and covered up to present a cohesive facade to the rest of the world. And it is that fabric facade - a Norman Rockwell canvas - that was ripped to shreds in New Orleans, Louisiana. The scene in the Convention Center - 25,000 people living in fear and feces - exposed America as a fraud.

The white reporters feeding their reports to white studio anchors felt like they were in a Third World country, or so they said. Who do they interview? Trent Lott, who said that he was pleased with the federal response to the tragedy. Even President Bush, never the sharpest blade in the tool box, has admitted that the results were unacceptable. Many reporters have called those throngs of devastated people "refugees." Refugees! If a similar tragedy occurred in Phoenix or Boston, would the reporters have called the displaced citizens refugees? I strongly doubt it.

They were faced with the knowledge that they had been left behind and, with no communication, forgotten and abandoned. People lost their homes, their business, their churches, and hospitals. They were immediately stripped of everything. And then, through inaction, the federal government stripped them of the last shreds of their dignity.

There was a three-day advanced notice. Three Days!! FEMA, the Federal Emergency Management Agency, should have been prepared. It's not as if this disaster was not anticipated. The previous year, FEMA ran a 5-day drill about a hypothetical hurricane named PAM hitting New Orleans. It was determined that the city could fill with water and that thousands could die. It was known that approximately 100,000 of the poor had no cars, thus, no way to evacuate the city. Despite the lessons learned in that drill, it took five days for large-scale deliveries of food, water, transportation and medical services to begin to arrive in New Orleans. That is absolutely criminal.

Give those pencil-neck bureaucrats enough time and they will come up with the appropriate excuses to explain their failure. By Saturday afternoon, six days after the hurricane hit, they have already begun to cover their own asses. In fact, had they been as quick to respond to the crisis as they are to scapegoat their incompetence, lives would have been saved.

Letter to the Editor:
Cruise Ships? Riiiight!

No surprise that the evacuees in the Astrodome refused to transfer to cruise ships. Historically, black people have heard that ol' cruise ship story before.

[Selected by the Atlanta Journal Constitution as Quote of the Week on September 11, 2005]

[Selected by the Atlanta Journal Constitution as Quote of the Year 2005, on January 1. 2006]

The Poverty of Spirit:
Katrina and The Holidays

(December, 2005) One of the realities unmasked by Hurricane Katrina is the way in which we look upon the misfortune of those who struggle from day to day under the cloud of poverty. We saw people – everyday, hardworking people – thrown into instant need and it hurt us on a personal level; perhaps more so than ever before. We saw ourselves with no food, no home, no water, or electricity. We saw life beyond living from paycheck to paycheck. We saw what life was like when the ATMs were closed and the banks catastrophically shut down – for days, then weeks, then months.

The reporters saw people without their wigs and make-up, and they pitied them beyond the concern that could have rectified the situation. We saw poverty on our TV screens - a poverty that was not poor. It was a need that did not dangle precariously from a shot glass or a syringe. No one knows your blues like you. No one knows your pain. That reporter can't live your blues, and doesn't want to anyway. He sees the struggle and calls it poverty. He sees survival and calls it looting. The poverty of 2005 New Orleans was a bankruptcy of spirit, but it was a bankruptcy that wasn't poor.

Poverty is a larger scale, third-world country, late night TV beg-a-mercial, "for the children" poverty. But Poor is more personal, more isolated - a day-to-day struggle to make it home. Poor is on a scale that no one really considers to be poverty. It's not destitute, or homeless. It's not soup kitchen, cardboard box needy. It's an ache from hollowness; a wanting of nothing more than not hurting anymore. It's driving on two tires with slow leaks and expecting a third, yet feeling relieved because you don't yet have a flat. Poor makes slow leaks your friends. It's the all-the-way flat tires that are conspiring against you. The slow leaks give you time… time to find the fifty-cents for the air machine (yeah, they've finally got around to charging us for air).

During the holidays, being poor is having few expectations and none of them good. It's listening to your phone ring again, and again… and again, then finally not caring who it is, because who ever it is wants something from you that you don't have. Caller ID is your get-out-of-jail-free card - God's way of balancing it all out, so that you get a breather now and then. And ever so often, God let's you pass by a trailer park and a mobile home with a Confederate flag in a window, just to let you know that you have not yet hit rock bottom.

Those who think the poor are ignorant should listen to the dialog that transpired for a Christmas tree, haggled over on Christmas Eve.

The poor may not know they are poor, but Christmas Eve can surely make you feel inadequate. Poor is coming home with anything… but nothing. And as the money gets tighter, it's your child looking into your eyes and making allowances for the lack of gifts. The only thing sadder than not having anything is your child saying it's OK.

Christmas remains special because it allows the rest of us to help, if we can. And we must help, because we now know that we are all just one well-placed Category 5 hurricane away from Poor.

Indifference - Another White Privilege

The most surprising aspect about the results of the latest Gallup poll on the widening gap between perceptions of blacks and whites is that anyone would find it surprising. As a black man, my views about America are shaped by my treatment in America. My personal experiences of racial profiling on several occassions behind a steering wheel in Marietta, for example, allow me to see this country from a different vantage point.

White privilege is a social blindfold that allows most whites to go through their day oblivious to the humiliation and disrespect meted out to minorities around them on a daily basis. When we complain, we're accused of harboring a victim mentality. I submit that a victim mentality is based on experienced victimization in a country mired in institutionalized racism.

Reincar-Nation

I'm not sure that I really believe in reincarnation, but if it actually happens, I have but one request. When I die I want to come back as a white man's pet. Dog or cat, it doesn't matter, because whites don't make the distinction. Their pets are part of the family, and they treat them royally. How many times have you heard a white person describe his/her pet as "baby?" How about those who even dress their animals in hats and clothes? Their pets even eat better than 40% of Americans, because they carefully prepare each nutritional portion. We found out how much whites care about the nutrition of our school children, back when Ronald Reagan declared that ketchup was a vegetable.

When you think about it, the closest that whites have ever come to actual slavery is pet ownership - where the pet is the master, and the white man is his slave. He feeds him when he's hungry. He indulges the dog's every whim. He walks him around until the dog poops and, lately, he even picks up Fido's shit and places it in a bag. I love seeing this, but I'm sure that whites don't recognize the slavery aspect of it all. Like all masters, at times the dog even slips away and sleeps in his slave's bed.

Thomas Jefferson, are you feeling me on this?

Now, I realize that black people have pets, too. When I was a kid, we had a dog, but he wasn't anybody's master. He ate what he could get, when he could get it. Nutrition? He'd chomp on the dining room table leg just because it was brown. He knew that scraps were a delicacy. I now understand that when he sat up on his hind quarters and lifted his two front paws, he was actually praying that when he died he' d come back as a white man's dog.

So after a lifetime of fighting The Man for every square inch of my existence, I'll be ready for a break. I'll be looking for reincarnation as a white man's pet. And I'll be taking all the fringe benefits, too. Yeah, I want to shit on his $10,000 area rug and pee on her Prada shoes. I want to jump up on their bed, sleep on their 2,000-thread count sheets, and wipe my ass on their pillows. I will do all of that as their pet, and they will smile, pat my head and happily submit as I plunge my doggie-breathed tongue down their throats.

It seems that some white people will endure anything, as long as they can attribute it to animal love. They treat people – even other white people – like shit, but they have all the love and respect in the world for animals.

OJ Simpson would be electrified dust right now if his murdered wife had been holding a little mutt when she was slain. Whites crucified quarterback Michael Vick for his involvement with dog fighting.

As far as I'm concerned, Vick couldn't shoot, drown or electrocute enough of those flea-bitten pit bulls for my taste. But there's one thing I know for sure - you don't fuck with a white man's dog. You can take his money. He will give up his car, his woman, his season stadium tickets, but don't mess with his dog. You don't want that kind of grief. Mike Vick is just beginning to learn that lesson.

The question, then, is WHY? My guess is that, throughout history, whites have exploited every other race of people on the planet, and animals are the only beings left that they trust not to be nurturing a grudge.

They may be right. I rooted for the shark in "Jaws."

I'm Dreaming of a White Christmas... Party

Well, it's that time of year. Christmas. Majority white business offices all over the country will be celebrating the holiday season with an Office Christmas Party. For me, it's the amusing time of year when the administrators at my job feel compelled to personally "invite" me to the company Christmas Party. It was only about ten years ago that I decided to stop blowing smoke up their asses with tales of "other commitments," and just tell them flat out, "NO!" This year, it was all I could do to keep from saying "HELL NO!" It's not as if they don't have a couple of other black employees to attend their party. And I suspect that those blacks feel pressured to do so, perhaps thinking that, if they didn't attend, it may reflect poorly on their performance reviews. But I have never understood why black people put themselves through it if they feel uncomfortable. A Christmas party has nothing to do with job performance, although I'm sure that some careers have been significantly shortened by a few drinks too many at an office party.

My Dad once advised me to never position myself between a white guy and a pitcher of beer. "You won't like the result," he suggested. What dear old Dad didn't understand is that, on a purely social level, as an adult, whites have never even shown up on my radar screen. So attending a holiday party with white co-workers has never entered my mind. Isn't a party supposed to be a social event at which one enjoys oneself? How could I enjoy myself while being stereotyped, disrespected and condescended to? There's something so contrived about people who endure stuff for the sake of appearance. Besides, I've found that some whites only want to be around us at this time of year because it makes them feel good about themselves. I'm supposed to attend a Christmas party so that a room full of tight-assed white folks can feel good about themselves? That must be straight out of the Ebeneeza Scrooge book of racial relations.

The thing that launched my anger this year was a decidedly new approach. One of the VPs approached me with an offer to send a limousine to pick up me and Tricia, and bring us to the Marietta Country Club for the Christmas Party, I chuckled to myself as I wondered if they planned to ask us to serve, as opposed to being served. So, in essence, we would be bused to their Christmas Party. The sweet irony in this is that their parents probably fought to their deaths against forced busing back in the 1960's. Of course, that particular Vice President - born and raised in the hills of Georgia - didn't even consider the offer to be insulting, and I was going to give him a pass... until he pressed me for an explanation as to why not, and suggested – half jokingly - that he might call my home and ask my wife. He explained that often the "little woman" can convince her husband to change his mind.

OK, so now the gloves are OFF!

I told him that the "Richard" he works with every day is merely a character I created in order to survive in this profession (engineering) as a black man for 39 years. "It's an act!?," he asked. I explained that Richard is a 40-hour-per week persona, who vanishes each day as I head home. Had I been in Kenyada mode, I might have mentioned that I would never even consider attending any social function with my co-workers, a bunch of right-wing Republican/Conservatives, whose idea of liberalism is a *white* lawn jockey. But I just let it stand at "Yes, it is."

I guess I'm just getting too old for this shit.

Cotton: The Fabric of Our... Oppression

Have you seen the latest cotton commercial? The cotton industry shows us acres and acres – horizon to horizon – of cotton fields, just ripe for the picking. With gentle piano/guitar music strumming softly in the background, you would think that they were hawking a romantic dinner in Shangri-la.

But when I see that commercial, I'm not seeing rows of cotton plant in its raw state. I'm seeing black folks dying of heat stroke and infected whip lashes, forced to pick the future fabric of our lives. Our ancestors toiled in cotton fields – perhaps some of the same cotton fields shown in the commercial. They toiled as slaves.

"It was work hard, git beatins and half fed... . The times I hated most was pickin' cotton when the frost was on the bolls. My hands git sore and crack open and bleed." –Mary Reynolds, Slave Narrative from the Federal Writers' Project, 1936-1938

In the 72-year period between the arrival of slaves in Jamestown, and the ratification of the Thirteenth Amendment prohibiting slavery, it is conservatively estimated that one million individuals were enslaved, either by transatlantic, or by domestic slave traders, for the production of cotton.

In 1820, the American Farmer, an agricultural magazine, estimated that a single slave could tend six acres of cotton and eight acres of corn. But by the time of the Civil War, slaves worked ten acres of cotton and ten acres of corn. For field slaves, this meant a life of hard labor from before sunrise until the late hours of night, for a never-ending work cycle. Slave labor was pushed onto those cotton fields to work. Those who had full strength worked on plow gangs. The weaker field hands – including most women, older men and children 6-12 years of age – worked the hoe-gangs. Some overseers allowed slaves to whistle or sing as they worked, but many did not allow slow singing, concerned that the work pace would slow down in rhythm with the music.

In 1850, at the height of the plantation system, almost three-quarters of the 2.5 million slaves in the U.S. were used in the production of cotton.

Slaves in the cotton fields were given a certain weight quota of cotton. Apparently, in those times whites weren't concerned about quotas. Punishment was severe for not meeting one's quota. In one slave narrative, punishment was described as one stroke of the bullwhip for every pound that is short of the task. And the number of whip lashes was graduated according to the nature of the "offence."

On one plantation, 25 lashes were inflicted upon a slave whenever a boll (cotton seedpod) was found in the cotton, or when a branch was broken in the field. Fifty lashes was the ordinary penalty following some slightly higher delinquencies. The more severe punishment of 100 lashes was meted out for the serious offence of standing idle in the field. And five hundred, well laid on lashes, in addition to the mangling of the dogs, is inflicted upon any slave who dared run away from the field.

So Cotton, Incorporated may want to rethink the latest attempt at advertising their product with a romanticized depiction of the cotton fields. Those fields are not looked upon in the same way by the descendants of the slaves who were forced to work them.

And we will never forget.

The APOLOGY, Part 2

My original essay, "The Apology" was written in 1997, and published on the Internet. From there, it was "borrowed" and adopted as the finale to a stage production of "The MAAFA Suite" by St. Paul's Community Baptist Church in Brooklyn, New York. The production received rave reviews and traveled all over the country to such cities as Dallas, Detroit, Chicago, Seattle, and Atlanta. In 2004, my wife and I were invited to attend the excellent New York production. Upon my return to Atlanta, I then published it as part of my first book, "Essays & Open Wounds While Waiting for The APOLOGY."

At the heart of my essay was a demand for an official apology from the government of the United States. Once again (with feeling), this is not about the people of the United States needing to apologize to African Americans and their descendants. First of all, African Americans and their descendants are also people of the U.S. The Apology for slavery should come from the President of the United States representing the government of the United States. As I stated in my book, "On some level, this is not even about white people. One entity enforced slavery through the power of law and the Constitution – from 1789 to the ratification of the 13th Amendment in 1865. I want the apology of the government of the United States of America."

On Tuesday, July 29, 2008, the U.S. House of Representatives used a voice vote to pass a nonbinding resolution that serves as a formal apology for the government's participation in African American slavery and the establishment of Jim Crow Laws. The term, "Jim Crow" comes from "Jump Jim Crow," a song and dance routine from 1828 that was performed in blackface by white comedian T.D. "Daddy" Rice, who was inspired by the song and dance of a crippled African in Cincinnati named Jim Cuff (or Crow). The song was a hit and Rice performed it all over the country as Daddy Jim Crow. That song was the first of a genre that sought to mock black people in song and dance, and led to minstrel shows, "Amos 'n Andy,' and "Home Boys in Outer Space."

Jim Crow Laws were enacted mostly in the Southern and border states between the 1870's and 1965. Under those laws, blacks were denied the right to vote and other civil liberties, up to and including legally separate facilities (like public restrooms and water fountains) from whites. Jim Crow tapped into every facet of life for blacks, from segregated schools and restaurants, to segregated public transportation and entertainment venues.

House Resolution 194 takes into account the Jim Crow Laws and how they affected day-to-day life for African Americans. Keep in mind that the apology was only officially acknowledged by the House of Representatives. The Unites States Senate declined to participate in a joint resolution, not that anyone ever dreamed they would. While several individual states have issued official apologies for slavery, this is the first time that a federal branch of the government has done so. The resolution, first submitted in February 2007, was authored by U.S. Representative Steve Cohen. Cohen is a white Congressman who represents a majority African American district in Memphis, Tennessee. It is important to note that the text of the resolution does not state that the U.S. Government apologizes for slavery. It sates that the House "apologizes on behalf of the American people..." as if we weren't, and aren't, American people.

The U.S. government continues its reluctance to accept blame for its role in slavery, most likely because that kind of admission might leave the government open to a class action lawsuit for fiscal reparations. So what we actually get with this resolution is a half-hearted sugar pill loosely veiled in denial. But it's a beginning.

Here now is House Resolution 194 in its entirety, so that we take full measure of both how much was said... and how little. Here's the text of the final resolution:

Whereas millions of Africans and their descendants were enslaved in the United States and the 13 American colonies from 1619 through 1865; (Engrossed as Agreed to or Passed by House)

House Resolution 194

In the House of Representatives, U. S., July 29, 2008.

Whereas millions of Africans and their descendants were enslaved in the United States and the 13 American colonies from 1619 through 1865;

Whereas slavery in America resembled no other form of involuntary servitude known in history, as Africans were captured and sold at auction like inanimate objects or animals;

Whereas Africans forced into slavery were brutalized, humiliated, dehumanized, and subjected to the indignity of being stripped of their names and heritage;

Whereas enslaved families were torn apart after having been sold separately from one another;

Whereas the system of slavery and the visceral racism against persons of African descent upon which it depended became entrenched in the Nation's social fabric;

Whereas slavery was not officially abolished until the passage of the 13th Amendment to the United States Constitution in 1865 after the end of the Civil War;

Whereas after emancipation from 246 years of slavery, African-Americans soon saw the fleeting political, social, and economic gains they made during Reconstruction eviscerated by virulent racism, lynchings, disenfranchisement, Black Codes, and racial segregation laws that imposed a rigid system of officially sanctioned racial segregation in virtually all areas of life;

Whereas the system of de jure racial segregation known as `Jim Crow,' which arose in certain parts of the Nation following the Civil War to create separate and unequal societies for whites and African-Americans, was a direct result of the racism against persons of African descent engendered by slavery;

Whereas a century after the official end of slavery in America, Federal action was required during the 1960s to eliminate the dejure and defacto system of Jim Crow throughout parts of the Nation, though its vestiges still linger to this day;

Whereas African-Americans continue to suffer from the complex interplay between slavery and Jim Crow—long after both systems were formally abolished—through enormous damage and loss, both tangible and intangible, including the loss of human dignity, the frustration of careers and professional lives, and the long-term loss of income and opportunity;

Whereas the story of the enslavement and de jure segregation of African-Americans and the dehumanizing atrocities committed against them should not be purged from or minimized in the telling of American history;

Whereas on July 8, 2003, during a trip to Goree Island, Senegal, a former slave port, President George W. Bush acknowledged slavery's continuing legacy in American life and the need to confront that legacy when he stated that slavery `was . . . one of the greatest crimes of history . . . The racial bigotry fed by slavery did not end with slavery or with segregation. And many of the issues that still trouble America have roots in the bitter experience of other times. But however long the journey, our destiny is set: liberty and justice for all;

Whereas President Bill Clinton also acknowledged the deep-seated problems caused by the continuing legacy of racism against African-Americans that began with slavery when he initiated a national dialogue about race;

Whereas a genuine apology is an important and necessary first step in the process of racial reconciliation;

Whereas an apology for centuries of brutal dehumanization and injustices cannot erase the past, but confession of the wrongs committed can speed racial healing and reconciliation and help Americans confront the ghosts of their past;

Whereas the legislature of the Commonwealth of Virginia has recently taken the lead in adopting a resolution officially expressing appropriate remorse for slavery and other State legislatures have adopted or are considering similar resolutions; and

Whereas it is important for this country, which legally recognized slavery through its Constitution and its laws, to make a formal apology for slavery and for its successor, Jim Crow, so that it can move forward and seek reconciliation, justice, and harmony for all of its citizens: Now, therefore, be it

Resolved, That the House of Representatives—

(1) acknowledges that slavery is incompatible with the basic founding principles recognized in the Declaration of Independence that all men are created equal;

(2) acknowledges the fundamental injustice, cruelty, brutality, and inhumanity of slavery and Jim Crow;

(3) apologizes to African Americans on behalf of the people of the United States, for the wrongs committed against them and their ancestors who suffered under slavery and Jim Crow; and

(4) expresses its commitment to rectify the lingering consequences of the misdeeds committed against African Americans under slavery and Jim Crow and to stop the occurrence of human rights violations in the future.

The resolution does not address reparations at all. In fact, the way in which certain passages are stated, such as, "apologizes to African Americans on behalf of the people of the United States, for the wrongs committed against them and their ancestors who suffered under slavery…"

It makes no mention of the Constitution of the United States, which governed the country beginning in 1789, and sanctioned slavery until 1865. How can the house apologize for the People when the government was the instrument through which slavery, the original sin, was allowed to flourish?

The Last White Guy in the White House

(August, 2008) Will the last white man in the white house please turn off the lights? Oh never mind! After eight years of George W. Bush, the lights are already out, we just didn't realize it. While it's true that the whites who elected him deserve what they got, I'm not sure that he should be the last Caucasian, the shoulders of whom should carry the legacy of all the white Presidents forevermore. This is America and even old white guys deserve better than that.

Of course, one could make the argument that they elected George W. Bush and nominated John McCain to replace him. John McCain? It was inevitable that sooner or later the Republican Party would run out of doddering old white men – or young white men with doddering old ideas. But who could have guessed that it would happen this soon, or this emphatically. John McCain is so old, and so pathetically ill-prepared for this campaign that I suspect he may get a sympathy vote. He is 72 years old in September. Even Ronald Reagan was only 69 when he became president. How desperate was the Republican Party when they looked around and decided that Father Time was the best suited Republican for the job. They've gone from Old White Men to

REALLY Old White Men. GOP used to stand for Grand Ole Party, now it's Geezers On Parade. It's a good thing that Republicans are famous for having no heart, or I'd really be worried about McCain's.

Don't get me wrong. I've always wanted Obama to win, but I expected a more formidable opponent than McCain. This is like the 1992 Dream Team playing against a bunch of slow, non-jumping white guys – with two-hand set shots and a prayer. Republican presidential campaign managers have their work cut out for them all right. They have to make John McCain seem fresh. The problem for Democrats is that McCain is not the ogre that George W. Bush is, So we lose the votes that would be cast *against* him, in lieu of the votes cast for Obama. I'd have no problem with McCain as a doting old grandfather, tucked away in somebody's back yard, under a shade tree in Florida. But as President of the United States? Old fella, please!

How many barrels of mediocrity do you have to scrape to come up with enough dregs to sculpt a John McCain? This shows you something about The Old White Men. They should have known that their chances were slim when McCain started winning primaries. He was standing up there on all those stages with a bunch of losers, and compared to them, McCain looked average. What does that tell you?

When retired Gen. Wesley Clark remarked that, "riding in a jet fighter, and being shot down was, in and of itself, not an accurate barometer of a person's fitness to be President," I stood up in my living room and applauded. Finally someone got real about John McCain. Even though the Republicans are crying foul, the general's comments did not in any way denigrate the former war hostage's service record. Truth is that a prisoner of war is not necessarily a war hero. McCain got shot down. Since when is mediocrity a cause for hero worship? Since when did the Republicans trade the John Wayne image for a pilot that bails out? Excuse me; given the choice, I'd prefer to vote for a jet fighter pilot who *didn't* get shot down.

John McCain will lose this election because he's just another Old White Man whose ambition exceeds his capability. Edged on by some yes-men who were a part of the entourage of puppeteers that propped up G.W. Bush for eight years, McCain is in way over his head.

WAKE UP! GET UP! WISE UP!

"Three years old, I fell off my tricycle. I started to cry and waited for my Daddy to pick me up. But he told me to stop crying, get up off the ground and pick up my tricycle. That advice worked for me then... and it works for me now."

Black Men in Crisis?

Ironically, in the aftermath of Black History Month 2006 – a celebration of our rich past of discovery, invention and accomplishment - there is a media buzz about the dire plight of today's young Black men. On March 20, 2007, a New York Times front page article by Erik Eckholm cited new studies by experts at major institutions that expose staggering statistics. But even beyond the numbers, these studies seem to sound a death knell for black men.

Once again, some black pundits have come out of the woodwork to denounce the bad news – not the stats, but the reporting of the stats on the front page in the New York Times. The impact of the message is being totally overlooked in favor of slaying the messenger. It's like the townspeople carrying torches to burn down Frankenstein's castle, and walking right pass the Monster.

The Monster in our story is not about the newspaper columnist, or the statisticians measuring our steps to the edge of the cliff. The Monster is the seed planted in our psyche 400 years ago that we are unworthy and incapable of living like men.

The employment and education statistics tell us that young black men have lost ground. Even in times of an economic boom and an overhaul of welfare, other groups - including black women - have made tremendous gains. That America keeps predicting our demise is more wishful thinking than razor sharp insight. While it is undeniably true that we are killing each other at an alarming rate, and we remain conspicuous by our absence from institutions of higher learning, there are solutions that are not being fully explored.

I keep hearing about the dwindling population of black men on the college campus, and the continued growth of black men in prison. I'm not too bright, so maybe I'm missing something in my assessment, but why not turn our prisons into educational institutions? If black men are there anyway, why not provide more books than exercise equipment? Sentence them to Education! Make them serve time, indeed; but make Time serve them, as well.

Our prisons should have the most extensive libraries in the nation, with volumes on American History, political science and law. There should be books about the humanities; books about family and civic responsibilities. There should be Dick-and-Jane books for those wanting to learn how to read. Black men in prison are a captive audience with much, much time on their hands. They don't need tenured professors, just something to do besides stare at three walls and bars.

For proof that educating the incarcerated can work, one needs to look no further than the true story of inmate Robert Stroud, a.k.a. The Birdman of Alcatraz. Stroud was an extremely violent man, who was convicted of murder and given a life sentence with no chance for parole.

Over the course of Stroud's thirty years of imprisonment at Leavenworth, he developed a keen interest in canaries, after finding an injured bird in the prison recreation yard. Since it was generally thought that allowing him to actually breed the birds would be a productive use of his time, prison officials let him construct two labs in adjoining cells. As he focused all of his time on the study of canaries, Stroud was able to author two books on canaries and the diseases that infect them. He raised nearly 300 birds, and became somewhat of an expert on the species. He even developed and marketed medicines for various bird ailments. In 1942, Stroud was transferred to Alcatraz Island where he remained until he died in 1963.

If prison is the final destination for the permanent underclass, then high school is the turning point of that journey. We must make our high schools a more compelling instrument for success by creating intermediate, small scholastic victories that our young black men can build upon. Our high schools need to be places where craft is as highly regarded as intellect. If young black men are interested in basketball and rap, teach them about the business of sports and the business of entertainment, and the intricacies of negotiating a sports or entertainment contract. We have a screwed up value system. The spotlight is always on those relatively few in front of the camera. The sanitation crews, police, and fire workers provide only a background canvas for the superstars. But the simple fact is that most of our young men - even if they are the cream of the crop - will become residents of that canvas. We need to encourage them to be the best they can be, regardless of the audience.

Twenty-five years ago, Time magazine said we were an endangered species. I did not buy it then, and I don't buy it now, but I understand the confusion. We, as black men, sometimes send out conflicting signals. Many of us have not been exposed to the best that we can be, to and for each other. We don't understand the mechanics of racism, and that a racist's best strategy is to make the indoctrination of the victim so complete that, ultimately, the victim victimizes himself.

There are few organizations beyond the African American family that can help us. Until recently, I have had little faith in faith-based institutions to find the solution. These days, no one is drinking the Kool-Aid except those who are already glazed over and sacrificed. But last Saturday, Tricia and I sat down to have lunch at a local restaurant. We were seated next to a table of 7 or 8 young black men. It appeared to be an informal meeting. They were talking about many things, but the conversation kept returning to issues of self help and responsibility. I soon gathered that it must have been some sort of mentoring program, and that maybe it was their first meeting. My guess was that it was connected in some way to a local church. It felt good to know that this sort of gathering is taking place, in light of all the dismal statistics.

The African American family and extended family have taken on many incarnations throughout our history. The one with which I'm most familiar is the African American family of GI's during the Vietnam War. Black men were in crisis during that war, but our strength was the way in which we handled it… together, as Brothers.

So don't tell me about Black Men in Crisis. I'm not accepting any excuses today. I've seen what we can be for each other in the worst of times. And I will never accept anything less.

Street Cred in Black America

It seems that every time I pick up a newspaper, there's a story about an important black sports star that is in deep do-do with the police. The latest is Falcons quarterback, Michael Vick, who was convicted for his connection to dog fighting. Of course, his troubles don't measure up to the murder charges that were faced by Baltimore Ravens linebacker Ray Lewis following a 2000 Super Bowl party. And since Lewis walked away from those charges, other football and basketball players have chosen to follow his footsteps onto the streets to hang out with homeboys from their old neighborhoods.

Someone needs to look into the black athlete's need to re-establish and reinforce street credentials with those who remain behind on the lowest rungs of the social ladder. Michael Vick's problem included relatives, not the least of which was a brother in desperate need of anger management classes.

Vick, a talented young football player lost everything due to his affinity for a permanent underclass mindset. Now he has cut his braids in an effort to change his image. Better that he cut his ties to relatives and others who don't have his best interests at heart.

To Be Young, Gifted, Black and HIV Positive

Ask a black person on the street about the major issues confronting African Americans today, and chances are the answers will range from the economy to high gas prices to racism. Rarely will HIV/AIDS be given as the answer. I can't figure out if we are just in denial or we're collectively that stupid that we don't know that our community is suffering through an HIV/AIDS epidemic.

We are so paranoid about the possibility of AIDS being known as a black disease, that we are ignoring the stats that tell us exactly that. Where it was once a disease that primarily affected gay white men, the face of AIDS has changed in the 25 years since the epidemic was first detected. Fifty-four percent of the new infections in the United States occur among African Americans. Sixty-four percent of the new infections in women occur in African American women. But heaven forbid we own up to the statistics.

Get over it!

HIV/AIDS IS A BLACK DISEASE! Hopefully, if we take ownership and end the denial, we can eradicate the disease. Even those of us who are not at risk… are at risk of spreading the disease by doing nothing to stop it. The Centers for Disease Control and Prevention is currently making an impact on educating the black community about the disease. It lists four challenges facing our community that impact upon HIV prevention – Poverty, Denial, Sexually Transmitted Diseases (STDs) and Drug Use. The agency has joined with politicians, black leaders, medical professionals and community-based organizations.

CDC studies show that undiagnosed HIV infection is responsible for over 50% of the new sexually transmitted infections each year.

For the past 15 years, the CDC has reported that the U.S. experiences an annual HIV infection rate of approximately 40,000, and half of them occur in people 25 years old or younger. Recently, it was reported that the annual infection rate is actually 40 percent higher than previously estimated. And if these new figures are accurate, then the CDC has under counted new infections by 15,000 per year for the last 15 years. This translates into roughly 225,000 more people living with HIV than previously estimated.

This new monitoring system is providing more accurate estimates of new infections than ever before available, particularly for specific populations. For example, infection rates for blacks were found to be seven times as high as for whites, and almost three times as high as for Hispanics.

The presence of AIDS in the black community is seen by some as the targeting of black people for extinction. Street corner historians always preface their conspiracy theories about AIDS with dibs and dabs about the Tuskegee Experiment. The true story is so unbelievably diabolical that the African American community's mistrust of anything connected to the medical industry is understandable.

For forty years between 1932 and 1972, the U.S. Public Health Service conducted an experiment on 399 black men in the late stages of syphilis. These men were mostly illiterate sharecroppers and they were never told what disease they were suffering from or of its seriousness. They were only told that they had bad blood. Their doctors had no intention of curing them of syphilis. The data for the experiment was to be collected from autopsies of the men, and they were deliberately left to degenerate under the ravages of tertiary syphilis—which can include tumors, heart disease, paralysis, blindness, insanity, and death.

In neighborhood barbershops, there was always some speculation as to the origin of AIDS in the black community. But as the disease began to take root on our streets, many blacks realized that it didn't matter whether AIDS found it's way to the community through gay white men, government planted infection, or a damn toilet seat – it's here now, and we'd better deal with it.

The black community must first take personal responsibility for its health and well-being. The government doesn't owe us anything that we don't owe ourselves, in triplicate. In the end, it doesn't matter how many programs the CDC initiates. It matters not how many government agencies get involved, or how many black leaders and politicians talk the talk. They can come up with all kinds of sophisticated scenarios, and solutions mapped out on legal pads. Action strategies sound great, tossed out across the conference room table. And deep down, everyone knows what needs to be done in order to turn the statistics around: practice abstinence, be monogamous and use condoms during sexual activity.

Nothing changes. Absolutely nothing changes until the HIV/AIDS epidemic is filtered down to the individual level and made a part of our everyday discussion – at our kitchen tables, in our family rooms and, most importantly, in our bedrooms. This is an African American health crisis that demands the attention of each of us – every man, woman and child. It needs to be a topic of discussion in every home, at every family reunion, picnic, barbecue and church social.

We must own the AIDS epidemic in much the same way in which we have come to own the National Basketball Association. Little black boys much too small to navigate their way across a busy street KNOW that they can play basketball. It's seen as a rite of passage; a natural law in the black community. They talk basketball. They dream basketball. They think basketball, and they have no doubt that they will be the NBA's next Michael Jordan. We need to help them acquire the same single-minded focus on their health, and the health of every member of their families. The challenges facing the black community begin and end with Education. We need to educate ourselves about HIV and AIDS prevention, on the front end of prevention, but we also need to educate ourselves about getting tested and exploring our options in the event we do test positive for HIV/AIDS. Half a million African Americans are now living with HIV, and blacks are 10 times more likely than Whites to have AIDS. Confronting this national health disparity is a paramount concern. But you can stack the studies like pancakes, with reams of reports and statistics to block out the sun. Blacks at the grassroots level need more than statistics and paperwork. Over 200,000

Black people have died of AIDS and we need to see a depiction of those AIDS deaths in every major city across this country.

There is a traveling Vietnam Memorial Wall with over 58,200 engraved names of dead soldiers. The Wall is transported all over the U.S., helping Americans to understand the price we paid in the war. Imagine the impact of two hundred thousand black mannequins, lined up along the centerline of 125th Street in Harlem, or Edgewood Avenue in Atlanta, representing the lives we have lost to AIDS. The disease is a thickening fog that hangs over our community with the promise of impending death.

It's time to take it personally and to Fight back.

Gun to Our Heads

As a nation of football fans, players, and the rest of us mourn the death of Washington Redskins star Sean Taylor, I feel compelled to again note the gun pressing against our collective temple. And the color of the trigger finger is black. Once again young black men fill the roles of both victim and murderer. And there are no apologies forthcoming for my political incorrectness. Where is Reverend Sharpton now? Yo' Jesse, where's the outrage?

The permanent underclass has declared war, and the rest of us haven't heard the news. We have busied ourselves with our work, our play and our stopped up sinks, while they have armed themselves for war. Their defense attorneys will argue that they kill because they are poor, black, angry and misunderstood, like it's a get-out-of-jail-free card for killing the rest of us who are poor, black, angry, misunderstood … and unarmed?

Unlike the mid-20th Century, the enemy is not wearing white hoods and swooping in under the cover of darkness with lighted torches and White Citizens Council membership cards. The enemy in our neighborhoods is not the Middle Eastern terrorist with a strapped on bomb and a misguided mission from Allah.

A black kid just shot and killed Sean Taylor... because he was there.

Black Privilege: A Sense of Entitlement to Anger

We have talked about White Privilege, the air of entitlement most whites are said to feel on a daily basis. They take for granted, for example, that they deserve a seat in the front row of life, by virtue of their existence. While White Privilege is a commonly accepted fact of life, Black Privilege – the sense of entitlement to anger, attitude and violence is quietly blanketed in denial and ignorance.

The entitlement implied by, and impregnated in, the new Black Privilege is not about Rolls Royces and bling-bling. We have raised a generation of young people who feel entitled to a rage that is not theirs to own, because it is rage one or two generations removed. It is rage anchored and authored by media. Reading about the Black Panthers, seeing a racially charged movie, or hearing about racism from a rap album, some young people feel entitled to strap on weaponry and look for someone to strike. And the person most likely to suffer their theatrical rage will be a real live black person.

Their lack of esteem dictates that you will most likely be the victim of their unteth ered rage. You talk about the Middle East with young people strapping bombs onto themselves and running into a bus. Young African Americans are strapping the bomb to themselves, and then assembling their closest friends and family members.

The entitlement to anger, attitude, and violence is often preceded by the entitlement to placing blame. No matter what happens, first look for someone to blame. Young people are quick to make excuses. Fail in school, blame the teacher. Get in trouble with the police, "they singled me out because I'm black." Get fired at work, "their requirements [like being on time, dressed for business] are unfair to blacks." Can't find a job, "the employers are prejudiced." Of course, there's no getting around it, white people and their racism are convenient, if not willing, targets. But at some point, we need to take an updated assessment and then be willing to accept our own complicity in the results.

The new Black Privilege is promoted by record companies in a Hollywood shuffle of looking for the next Snoop Dogg. Mostly white, they have a concept of disenfranchised black youth. They'll take any kid with a 25-word vocabulary and an attitude, and make him a star. This festering virus in our consciousness can only thrive in a void of leadership – both at home and on the national stage. When did a prison term become a badge of honor, and assisting the police a dishonorable act of black treason? Our world has become topsy-turvy, when it used to be just off-center. We have become bottom-heavy, overloaded by under-achievers, with rappers commandeering the podiums, and serious leaders reduced to current events groupies.

We are now reaping the consequences of the seeds we have sown. Preaching civil rights without preaching civil responsibilities is irresponsible. The debt owed by The White Man - the entire white race – pales by comparison. The greatest debt owed in the aftermath of slavery is the debt we owe ourselves. And that does not excuse them. It's just saying that ultimately the responsibility is ours.

Years ago, some of us apparently thought that the thug initiative was cute as entertainment or a curiosity. But now, as it creeps closer and closer to the center of black consciousness, the worry has set in. Must we always be late to the party in order to fancy ourselves as having "arrived?" If the pain is ours, so too must be the relief for that pain. It's time that we own both. Our leaders - if in fact there are any left - should not only be articulating the message, they should be shaping it. They should not only be painting the landscape; they should be planting it. There is a price tag attached to sticking our collective head in the sand. But it is costly, immediate, and self-destructive.

We've got to do something because if we don't resolve the issues of Black Privilege, we won't have to worry about White Privilege. We won't have to worry about The White Man at all. He will have moved on to something more challenging than a race of people who are self imploding. And in the end, when the Epilogue is written, we will not have been betrayed by the thug culture, or its anger, attitude and violence; we will have been betrayed by our own silence.

Internet Discussion:
Black Rage & Anger

In the wee hours of the morning, two African American males - a 22-year old and a 52-year old - sit down for a chat across the kitchen table known as The Internet.

Umoja: Why is young Black Rage and Anger so hard to understand for our elders? Kenyada, I found myself meditating on two of your archived articles (1. Tupac & 2. Khallid Muhammad)... and I just feel led to talk about them. I understand your responses (and I feel ya)

But I also know what it's like to be the militant on campus... the "bringer of hate/anger"... I'm a recent college Grad, 22 years of age (probably real close to your son's age)... and I, my fiancé, and our 2 best friends were the BSU officers.

In those posts, we faced so much from so many... because we didn't want the few black students on campus tap dancing for the masses, whites were mad... because we didn't put Black & White unity first on our agenda, many professors found us out of place and not useful in a de-segregated society"

Our goal was simply Black Love First... when we arrived on campus with just a hundred black people... there was no black unity, nor black studies program... even sisters and brothers weren't talking... my fiancé and I were the first black couple...

And as I grew in that relationship, and knowledge of history... I understood that I had a reason to be mad... because so many of us had been tricked, and therefore had become complacent. Many of my classmates hated themselves and hated me for trying to inform them. They were afraid to say to white people what needed to be said. They did not want to be thought of as Black (rather, earthlings)... I had a responsibility to speak when no one would or could; to act when no one would... to write when no one would... to raise hell and fight when no one would. It wasn't a responsibility to them, but to my ancestors and to my God to liberate myself and others from oppression. To appreciate myself... to love myself and others like me, and to never forget that it wasn't just Martin, but Malcolm too; that it wasn't just McLeod, but Davis too. That it wasn't just Booker, but David Walker too...

I think that sometimes we assuage the anger of youth by not saying, "Yes you have the right to be angry... you deserve it... let's try and fix the problems without taking less then we deserve." I think young Black Militancy can be informed, educated and articulate given the right opportunity and environment. It doesn't mean that people won't compromise... rather, they are not going to be walked upon.

Kenyada: Some younger people (not you) talk about Black Rage as if it's something that they invented. Do you not believe that there was rage in Dr. King? Hell yes there was! There was black rage even in the actor who played Stepin Fetchit, believe it or not. However, the rage that we see exhibited by many of today's youth centers on empty rhetoric and profiling. And often it is a rage that turns on blacks. In other words, it is self-destructive. When Khallid Muhammed incited a crowd of youth to riot against heavily armed NYC police, was that constructive ...or suicidal? Black folks don't need anymore martyrs, real or imagined. We need to take that rage and channel it in a positive direction. All that is important is that we live together in peace. That should be the goal. I support "Black Militancy" only when it is about more than empty anger. Black Militancy without commitment is ...a facade. Black Militancy without an education of one's history is ...stage acting.

What we found in the 60's was that there was a hard-core political activism that was community-based and committed to change. When they run movies and documentaries about the Black Panthers, for example, they show you the anger and the guns and the rhetoric. But I was around when it was about setting up neighborhood schools, and feeding the kids breakfast and lunch. Yes, they were full of rage, but they fed off of that rage to get the energy to do what needed to be done in the community.

That's where I'm coming from; that's where the seeds for my organization, Mr. Kenyada's Neighborhood (MKN) and PCs to the People were planted. That's also why I have no time or patience for "angry" young people who can only talk about "revolution" when they've got a joint dangling from their lips... or the appropriate rap music lyric in the background. REAL commitment is sobering; real constructive rage is not a sometimes thang; it's 24/7 ...liiiiive!!

I applaud young people who are out there "doing it", working in the community on a small scale; anonymous, but dedicated. I understand your sentiments and the "fire" you brought to your campus. But let me pass on a little of what I've learned, even at my advancing years, from working in the community. You can't be angry for someone else, anyone else. You can't spread your rage around with the hope of enraging others. All you can effectively do is to state your case - clearly and succinctly. Some will get it, some will not. Work with those who "get it." They will usually bring something of their own to the table, and together you may capture the imagination of others who get it. Bottom line ...work with those who get it, even if you know that it will benefit many of those who don't.

Every great man and woman of color understood that. And it's up to the rest of us to work with each other for the betterment of *both* of our races - African and Human.

Umoja: I agree with that philosophy. It is important to work... and I guess it's true that I've forgotten that even my elders are angry. I realize that you have a right to be angry, too. Although, so many times I find my elders acting out of complacency (not to say that my generation is any better).I know that anger should beget community involvement. Especially for the young (which have historically been the conspirators of change)... but how?.. and where?... and with what money?..

Remember the article in Newsweek... about the guy who had two kids, a wife, and a low paying job but, who was committed to the community... Although, his actions are applauded many of my sisters & brothers (my age) don't want to be caught in that low income rut for the sake of helping the community... I know that our generation has been ingrained with a hedonistic philosophy... but I know that many of us are educated and aware of the problems at hand...

But how do we balance that with our monetary needs? Take for instance Atlanta, where does one get a job working for the community where he/she can make enough money to support a car, home, and school loans? I haven't found one yet!!!!

Many of us want to do something, but we don't know how... and we don't know the means... When we think about it, we are amazed at the 50's-70's... because we can't really imagine what happened... and many of our parents don't want to talk about it because of the mental, physical and emotional trauma. I don't think we really have the tools to mobilize and act... Society has changed so drastically... and unfortunately our leaders have not, and our methods haven't either... so many of them (the methods) make us nostalgic for a period we really don't understand... In essence, I'm just trying to say... yes you are right...

but what do we do now... that's the answer I'm looking for. What do we do to empower and activate the soapbox rhetoric we articulate?

Peace and Blessings

Kenyada: Everything must change ...

The ways in which we deal with our adversaries; our concept of community activism; our desire to "change the world' before we change our own backyards.

It's interesting that you mention that our methods and leaders have not changed. That's one of my pet peeves; we're still marchin' and singin' while groups like the Southeastern Legal Foundation have given white racism an element of sophistication and respectability. There are no more dogs and fire hoses. Instead we are confronted by court challenges to affirmative action programs. These groups are well-funded, well-organized, well-connected. They are using the Internet, while we are using word-of-mouth. They are inside the courtroom using the justice system, while our leaders are *outside* the courtroom leading marches, holding hands, singing.

Everything must change.....

I would suggest that young people first secure a good education and pursue a career of their choice. You can't help anyone until you secure your own "footing". I'm an engineer, and it's a job that I *love*. It's my passion, and I'm lucky enough to get paid to do it. In addition to that, however, there is a need to help others. All through my career, I've tried in some small way to help younger people succeed in the engineering profession. I didn't try to change the world, as we know it, I just worked one-on-one, to do what I was capable of doing. Often young people want to paint the community activism portrait in broad-brush strokes, when small detail work is better accomplished.

In the beginning of MKN, I caught some flak for narrowing our focus on two major issues, computer literacy and teen pregnancy prevention. People wanted us to do "everything", everywhere ...for everyone. Whites said we were too exclusively pro-black in our focus. Some young blacks felt that the MKN concept should be "franchised" around the country instead of just within the boundaries of a small part of metro Atlanta. But I felt if we were to have any real, measurable success, we would have to concentrate our efforts right here in our own backyard ....first. We didn't want to change the world; we wanted to show the world how to change itself.

Another important lesson I've learned is that no matter how well intentioned your motives are, you cannot do it alone, and you shouldn't have to. Find a forum of like minds, and divide the responsibilities. Otherwise you will suffer "burnout' early on. It is possible to be selfless, without being self-sacrificing.

Peace

Battered Woman Syndrome

Recent back-to-back fatal incidents of domestic violence in an African American neighborhood of Atlanta prompted an Internet discussion. In one incident, a petite young woman, 17, was the mother of three - 5-month old twin daughters by her current boyfriend, and a two-year old from a previous relationship. Her boyfriend, 22, was becoming increasingly jealous and obsessed with her. He told her that she couldn't go to school or have a job, because he didn't want to share her with other people. He went as far as to hide behind trees in the couple's neighborhood to watch her.

She had been dating him for about 16 months and during the course of that time, he often threatened her and sometimes hit the small woman. Her family said that she mistook control for love. To her credit, she wanted to break off with him. Finally, the incidents escalated to him threatening her with a knife. Police said that the boyfriend stabbed the young woman, attacking with such force that he nearly decapitated her.

Clarice: Domestic Violence appears to be at an all time high lately, and seems to be increasingly more gruesome. I know I'm preaching to the choir, but please, please, mothers of young daughters, make sure your daughter knows that it's not cute and it's not flattering, and it's not a game, when some guy exhibits jealousy and possessiveness and other obsessive and controlling behavior toward her.

Rachel: Amen! I recall a conversation that I had years ago with my youngest sister. She expressed that she was flattered that her boyfriend was jealous and always wanted to know her every move....gosh, golly, gee...that obviously meant that he LOVVVVVVVVVVVED her! I think that we are seeing a very high incidence of young women who are so desperate for attention that they are willing to accept (and sometimes expect) maltreatment from their men. It's so prevalent that some people aren't even upset or disturbed by it anymore.

I certainly agree that we have to teach our girls to love themselves, but I would like to go a step further. We need to teach our young men that the measure of a man is not how badly he can beat his woman. We've spent decades trying to solve male/female relationships by using a unilateral approach of putting all of the responsibility on the woman.

We've totally left the offenders out of the picture when it comes to solving what is essentially THEIR problem. Stay with me now... When a woman is raped, folks want to ask (like they did when Mike Tyson was accused of rape) why did she go to his hotel room? I don't care if she went into his room butt naked, no one has a right to touch you without your permission.

I still cannot recall hearing many people saying why did he think that he could force someone into having sex with him? It took several misdeeds for folks to finally see what type of man he really was. I won't even get into the Robin Givens mess.

Or if a woman is beaten, they want to know what did she do to provoke him? Not why does he feel he has the right to put his hands on her? It's really twisted and until we bring young men into the dialogue, nothing will ever change.

Clarice: You're 200% correct that our young men need to be taught some very serious and important lessons on this issue. Moreover, it is really frightening when you realize that, for the most part, there is no one [or very few people] to teach them. Yes, mothers can do their best to teach them, but the harsh truth is that it takes a MAN [not just a male with specific body parts!] to raise a man! There are way, way too few of those around!

And, of course, once again it becomes business as usual and the major responsibility falls back to women to keep themselves safe from those predators.

My heart just bleeds for the 17-year-old mother of THREE! Now everybody is on camera talking about how he acted, but meanwhile, it does not appear that ANYONE took any logical steps to try to prevent the situation. It just seems to me that an idiot who hid behind trees, followed her, constantly scoured the neighborhood [on a bicycle, no less!] until he found her, didn't want her to go to school, and threatened her with a knife, should have been shut down long before he decapitated her. Was ANYBODY paying attention or did they all mistake it for "love?!"

Rachel: It does take a MAN to raise a son and you are right... there's no way a woman alone can adequately raise a boy to be a man. Unfortunately, there are too few men like the ones on this discussion board so this problem won't go away anytime soon. And about that poor 17-year old... More likely than not, they probably thought it wasn't their business so they stayed out of it. Tragic!

Terrence: Rachel, I agree with your intent, but your perspective concerns me a bit. Now let me be the first to acknowledge that we are at ends to find a remedy with domestic violence, so I can understand you wanting to caution your sister about some guy who is showing signs of possessiveness. However, let's remember how flattering this was for all women years ago before the domestic violence saga took off. It meant the guy was being for real when he displayed such a genuine attachment to her. You take that out of the picture and you have her looking to guys who just take her for granted with her thinking that's ok.

Maybe a better lesson to teach her would be to focus on how he treats other people. He may be the perfect gentleman with her but an asshole with others. Of course, that may be something she views as manly, thinking she'll always be excluded from it. Now is the time when you should be telling her it's not ok to be with an asshole, and not after she ends up butt naked in his bedroom screaming NO! Of course she only went there because this perfect gentleman asshole who never displayed any jealousy proposed marriage to her – later on of course. I doubt Robin Givens ever gave Mike Tyson a reason to be jealous and I'm sure Mike was the perfect gentleman long enough to dispel any doubts in her mind about what was coming. However maybe if she had considered how he treated others then she could have then put 2 +2 together and (along with a lick of common sense) avoided the inevitable.

Rachel: OK, something got twisted here... My perspective is fine. I think you are getting confused about what I said. My comments about my sister had nothing to do with rape. Also, it wasn't a post that was totally about my sister. I was giving at least three different scenarios in which I attempted to make a point about a man's possessiveness. With my sister, I was trying to explain how young women interpret a man putting them on lockdown (so to speak) as flattering... when actually it is far from it. Like I mentioned before, this was a while ago.... twenty one years to be exact... she's now forty. You're speaking like I had this conversation with her last week. Perhaps, this is where the confusion began? lol

Now to respond to your comment about "how flattering this was for all women years ago before the domestic violence saga took off." I have to take issue with you there. Firstly, you cannot speak for ALL women. I'd venture to say that you could really speak for none. You may be able to argue your point by saying SOME women, but there is no way for you to be able to declare that all women felt that way... no more than I can speak for ALL men... that would be preposterous! I would guess that if a woman did feel that way it would be because she needed to feel special or looked after until she got smart and realized that she was simply being controlled. Not ALL women are wise enough to see that at first... usually it takes years of manipulation and control for them to see through the B.S. There's a world of difference in showing 'genuine concern' and "sweatin' you". Every time this subject comes up, I'm one of the first to say that women need to be schooled on how to recognize these vipers for what they are. Unfortunately, the smooth talkers are just that and not every woman can see through the B.S. It's usually after experiencing a few bad apples that a woman learns how to spot them and if she passes this info along to the younger generation she's usually accused of being a bitter man-hating bee-otch when she is simply talking about a segment of the male population. Men can similarly testify about the female counterpart... because they DO exist! As far as Robin is concerned, I don't recall hearing anything negative about Mike before their marriage. But then again, I'm not really into boxing... so there could have been rumors about him being a beast. But who can say for sure when a batterer becomes a batterer. I don't believe you are born that way. I believe it is learned behavior... and someone has to be their first victim... perhaps she was. I do remember when she admitted what he had done on national television she was called everything but a child of God. Who knew after that interview that Mike would somehow become the 'victim'? Now, that's funny!

Unfortunately, there are no guarantees in life. You enter a relationship with hope… you try to put past demons to rest and look at your new partner for who he/she is. No one is a mind reader… the best that you can do is to get the hell out when s/he starts to act like a fool. In closing, watching how people interact and treat others isn't a foolproof way to determine if someone is sane. Think about all the neighbors who declare that the local mass-murderer was a sweet, gentle soul. Evil isn't always nicely packaged to mirror your usual garden-variety slasher film. It's insidious and subtle…to berate a woman because she's as telepathic as Ms. Cleo or has the investigative skills of Inspector Clouseau is simply unfair. It may be more helpful to try to get the criminals to stop committing crimes than to put a woman down for being a survivor.

Kenyada: Yes, we must raise our daughters not to be victims, but we should also raise our sons not to be perpetrators. Early childhood intervention will direct our boys to a different direction. Violence doesn't suddenly materialize in a teenager, as we all know. It is a learned behavior. Fathers need to understand the psychological messages they send their sons, with their language and with their actions. We all need to be on the same page if we are to stem the tide of domestic violence in our community.

Rosaline: You know I agree, but it's just like when our mothers used to talk to us girls about sex and pregnancy: Yes, the boys bear some responsibility, but they ain't the ones left holding the bag, so to speak. With domestic violence, it's usually NOT the guys who end up dead or maimed. Until we see more of that happening, no one is going to seriously consider turning the tide. Very much like drugs and alcohol. You all will recall that as long as drugs were confined (for the most part) in the 'ghetto,' it was never a problem. It wasn't until drugs found their way into suburbia and the boardrooms did we declare "war on drugs," and determine that it was time to create "rehab facilities" and the like. By the same token, do you think for a minute that if the world wasn't full of old white men there would be Viagra?! I mean, folks are dying by the millions from cancer and somebody comes up with a way to…

[Somebody stop me before I hurl myself in front of a large SUV!]

Kenyada: Unless the problem is confronted with our young boys, women in their future will continue to be maimed and killed. The "old white men" theory works in some cases, but domestic violence is something that we can handle in our own homes, with our own children.

Sheila: I know this is preaching to the choir, but where are the warriors? Even though I am at a crossroads about my girl Pearl Cleage at this moment, I am mindful of what she has said in the past about our community. I know violence is out there, but where are the warriors. For once in my life, I would like not to have to have this conversation because I know somebody's got my back.

Glenn: And how are we supposed to do that? How can, and why should, anyone take the responsibility for the behavior for that man that killed that young girl? Or that man who shot his wife in her front yard, or for the man that was the subject in the testimonial of one of our dear sisters. How? I would like to hear Pearl Cleage explain that to me. Society wants to place blame on any and everyone except where it squarely should be placed... on the perpetrator. I'm not going to be held accountable for anyone's actions but my own, and my responsibility does not extend to everybody who happens to share this world with me. I'm sorry, but her comment enraged me a little.

Sheila: I'm at a loss for words... almost

"Or that man who shot his wife in her front yard".

Be omni-present. Be omni-present in our lives and in our communities. My grandfather was omni-present. Everyday, everyone in my neighborhood knew that down our street there were men who were omni-present. Mr. Porter, Mr. Ivory were always working in their yards. My grandfather, everyday, walked the block. After that he sat on the porch when time for neighborhood children to come home from school. If so-and-so's car didn't pull in their drive way at a certain time or God forbid somebody's porch light didn't come on, he would go looking. If he had to go looking, other men would meet him at the end of the driveway. Also, we had keys to everyone's house and they had keys to ours. If they were to be late, he'd send one of us to turn the lights on. If one of us kids were late coming over the hill from school, half the neighborhood would come looking, and you'd better have a good reason for it. I would like to know that today, if by chance, my path were to cross a psycho obsessive that someone would come looking for me. I would like to know that there is no chance that someone could hide behind the trees in my neighborhood. I would like to know, that if a day would come that I don't make it home to my children, that there is someone out there who cares enough to notice. If there are men who are not willing to take on that responsibility, then I hope…

Terrence: I'll have to side with Glenn a bit on this one. I'll start with the women. It seems that even when women admit they are tired and trying to make ends meet that they ignore the main repercussions behind what drives them to even entertain the profile of the hustlers, bad boys and Mr. Excitement types that get them into these situations to begin with. No one seems to focus on the tendency of these women to walk out of one bad relationship just to end up with more bad company. They often seem to think that if a guy has a reputation where, "Oh, ain't nobody gonna mess with him" or "He drives a this and he drives a that" then he's going to be a good provider or protector and that the women in question will always be excluded from their wrath. It's moral insanity on the part of these women and these guys take full advantage of it. Address that!!!!

Now for the men… Like I said, I side with Glenn to a point. One thing that gets lost in looking at child raising is the concept of individualism. It's like we think all kids are born the same until they learn something from somebody else and then take off with it. I contend that's a bunch of crap!!!

Kids are born with different temperaments from the start and what they do with the information they receive is always going to be different from one child to another. We as parents are too often ready to take all the responsibility when a child comes out right but then we put our hands in our face and our thumbs up our ass when they don't. We just don't show enough open appreciation for kids making that decision to do the right thing despite whatever is going down around them. We need more Kenyada types to perpetuate this in more areas.

Now don't get me wrong, we need to give direction and support to our kids more now than ever. If we don't, somebody else will. We've rallied against prayer in school, but yet we allow sex and violence to dominate TV. We sit there with wine in hand and tell our kids not to do drugs. We condemn parents who spank but put under-aged kids in jail. I just can't figure out what the mental block is, when some of us are confused by a kid who doesn't learn about consequences until he's 21. Not all kids have it in them to need a strong introduction to this and it's more about their personal moral make up than it is those vain individuals trying to pass themselves off as super parents. It's not a pretty perspective but let's keep it real, folks. It hard for a tiger to change the stripes he's born with. Nothing to do with somebody giving them to him. All that said, I don't think looking at the child raising solution is appropriate given the assumption that we're trying to stop trouble before it starts. I think it's good to look at behavioral patterns and try to curb them or find an alternative release for them, but it really is no small order and it's a commitment by specific parents of specific children to take on. That's where the focus and support should be. You can't build a bully, a rapist or a criminal out of an otherwise normal child. Only extreme circumstances can evoke what may be perceived as criminal such as stealing for food or retaliation from being abused can drive a normal child there.

Looking at these extremes of personality alterations would give us a better perspective on what's needed to put into such a grand endeavor as turning a child around for the better. I can tell you that yelling from the podium ain't gonna get it. Everybody's tired. Most of those who aren't, only put up where it's convenient. It's one thing to criticize and say what needs to be done, but it's all quite another to look at it square in the face and see it for what it is and still be willing to participate in yours as well as anyone else's responsibility, having realized what a truly tall order it really is. It matters not that you've raised 10 successful kids. Only the man or woman who has successfully turned at least one child around (boy, girl, man or woman) has the answer.

Rachel: This may sound like I'm male-bashing, but judging from the little that I see... it appears that there aren't enough men to step up to the plate. I see so many TIRED sisters just trying to make ends meet and raise their families while the fathers are out in the street making more babies and ignoring them. Of course, the easy answer is to tell the women that they should be more selective about who fathers their children (with which I absolutely agree!)... but there needs to be a deep dialogue between the men... and other MEN about how their behavior is negatively affecting the future of our people.

Things were never this bad when I was growing up... most men took care of their children... it wasn't nirvana... but it was a rare occurrence for a FATHER to be referred to as a "Baby Daddy" or "Sperm Donor". I don't think the same thing can be said for today. When a father is absent, the result can be found in the prison system, on the street corner and in the graveyard.

When discussions get rolling they often slip away from the main topic. This discussion was no different. But we were not prepared to be emphatically dragged back to the topic of domestic violence when a member of our group made a startling revelation that, all at once, made the issue personal.

A Personal Story – The Battered Woman in the Mirror

Sonia: It's also about the signs... the indicators of that insidious disease, Battered Woman Syndrome. Lemme see... it wasn't a big deal when he wanted to know my every move. Kind of amusing, actually. I could handle it. No problem. Even joked about it with a couple of friends. OK, then he cut the telephone cords when someone called me. That wasn't amusing, but no need to panic. Saw someone else for dinner, we'd broken up by then, but still no grave matter when I got home, and he was waiting in the parking lot. It became a little more serious when he bashed my head against my front door and took my keys, but I still didn't tell anybody.

Later, after the rape and beating (not in that order), finally got the message and called the police -- after I hid his .357 when he fell asleep. Of course, when the police arrived, I just wanted to be left alone. No charges pressed, they couldn't determine that I was bruised (I'm not white, bruises don't show up that easily), no harm, no foul. Oh yeah -- begged me to get back together. Syndrome says 'hey -- you can still handle this, you're an enabler, a fixer, it'll be alright. Go ahead. YOU CAN FIX THIS.' "Fixing" now involves getting beaten regularly, having granted prior permission.

Now trying to hide total devastation from everyone. Got mad at my friend who figured out enough to call my mom and alert her that something was wrong. Didn't really wake up until I was almost dead the night of the Big Three -- kidnapping, beating and rape. OK, OK, OK -- realized I'm dealing with a complete madman. Can't fix this. But this is TOO humiliating. Who's gonna believe this? Doesn't matter, 'cause now he's stalking me. Talked to my pastor, who was his pastor (met him in church, y'know). Pastor says OK, just get an attorney and NEGOTIATE -- that way you won't damage his career.

Actually, that "pastor" saved my life. I left his office, went to the parking lot and turned out onto Memorial Drive -- and didn't stop until I got to the police station to file a report and swear out a warrant. We take our positive and negative motivation where we can get it.

Oh -- about the court thing. Knew it wouldn't be easy, but now a little courageous. Rape trial? Someone I dated who's by now violated the restraining order? No thanks. Let's stick with the misdemeanors. Now the DA is on my back, like he knows what it'll be like to be a defendant as much as this scumbag (growing a little stronger, now in therapy -- yep, he's a SCUMBAG!). A year and two prosecutors later, jury convicts him on all four counts, no jail time -- but I'm happy, 'cause if he went to jail it'd be for only enough time for me to fear for my life once he got out. Whew!

Battered women have to be worked with and worked on. They're silent. They don't like attention drawn to them. That makes them easy prey. They're co-dependent enablers who think they're so deficient no one else will have them. They put on a good front. They're good liars, and you can't call them crazy. Heck, they already know they're crazy. For the ones who manage to survive, it's almost an accident, but you can be sure that unless help is coming, they'll return to a relationship in which battering or emotional abuse will occur. (Or they'll let their CHILDREN emotionally abuse them...) And if they don't return to a batterer, they'll settle for the emotional abuse, 'cause after all "at least he doesn't hit me".

In the world of predators we live in, we've got to ratchet up the education of our young women as much as we need to look for signs in our young men. That way, looking for signs of BWS in women won't be such a cat-and-mouse game.

Mega Church Preachers: All That Glitters...

As Rev. Creflo Dollar and Bishop Eddie Long prepare to defend and justify their ultra lavish lifestyles as perks that go with the territory,

I welcome such scrutiny of the megachurch. For far too long, self-anointed Prophets of Profit have built monstrous structures - some might call it steeple envy - with an eye on bottom-line ticket sales referred to as tithes. And on Sunday evening, they return home to an oasis of excess such as Rolls Royce cars, private jets, and solid gold plumbing.

Surrounded by foreclosures and unemployment checks, one might wonder if these preachers can only hear the word of God. For their sake, I hope that God has a sense of humor.

[Selected by the Atlanta Journal Constitution as Quote of the Week, on November 9, 2007]

Do Something!
How I Became a Community Activist

In the 1972 blockbuster film, "The Poseidon Adventure," we saw actors Gene Hackman and Ernest Borgnine portray two characters that are drawn on classic Hollywood white male heroes. The cruise ship capsizes and a group of desperate people fight to survive. Hackman (the preacher) and Borgnine (the hardnosed ex-cop) are each trying to assume the leadership role. They each accept the challenge and stand ready to lead the survivors to safety. I loved this movie, because I always applaud people - white or black - who are willing to step into the role of leader. What we need in our communities are men who are drawn on the heroic characters of black history. Men who are capable of recognizing a need, and planning a strategy to meet the challenges we face as a people. I've always believed that, but I never saw myself in a leadership role... that is, until The Digital Divide statistics made headline news.

What is a leader? If I challenged you to find one in your own community, where would you go? Confronted with the very same challenge in 1997, I searched desperately for a political representative, or head of a civil rights organization, or even a faith-based group dedicated to helping people in times of crisis. But I could find no one - no leader with an e-mail address, and no leader who understood that the so-called Digital Divide represented a potential crisis in the African

American community. So I reluctantly decided to stand up and get involved. That was thirty years after I returned from two tours of duty in Vietnam, guilt-ridden for returning without a scratch when so many had made the ultimate sacrifice. A wise old man suggested that my life was spared for a reason, and that I needed to stop feeling sorry for myself, and find my destiny. The search ended with Computer Technology. I would lead in the promotion of computer literacy in my own community. If this was indeed why I was spared, then I was behind schedule, and it was time to get to work.

Have you ever wondered what goes into the making of an activist? I have often questioned how those who choose to step forward, find a way when, seemingly, there is no way. Well, I guess I found out. At that point, I was an engineer with 30 years experience in planning and construction. In that field, we begin with a foundation, and we built a structure. But as any engineer knows, before the foundation and the structure, you need a plan.

My plan was simple – bring computers and computer literacy to the African American community. When asked, I used only those ten words to describe a plan that would change people's lives. The crucial part of the plan was collecting data and information – the nitty-gritty research of what Vanderbilt University 1997 study called "The Digital Divide." I copied the statistics, but I also wanted to know about the attitudes and perceptions behind the stats. At each and every step of the way, I was unsure, frightened and intimidated by the challenge. But at each and every step of the way, I was surrounded by a supportive nucleus of friends who would not let me fail. At the height of our success, I knew that I owned the challenge we had adopted only three years earlier. And when Bellsouth asked me to create computer classes for them... I figured that it may be the only affirmation I would ever receive.

Ten years after launching my own non-profit organization dedicated to promoting computer literacy, getting computers into the homes of disadvantaged children, and free computer training to senior citizens... I received the following letter:

Mr. Kenyada,

My name is Shani and in May of 2000 I won your essay contest as a junior at Avondale High School. I wanted to let you know that your philanthropy has indeed changed my life. In 2001, I finished high school first in my class. I went on to attend Agnes Scott College where I earned a bachelor of arts in Economics and graduated Magna Cum Laude in three years. From there, I entered the hallowed halls of jurisprudence at the School of Law at the University of Georgia. I finished my studies and was awarded a jurist doctorate degree on December 13, 2006. I will attend graduation May 19th .

First I wanted to thank you for the computer. It indeed came in handy when I was at Agnes Scott. However, it wasn't the computer that's made the largest effect on me. Seeing the way you chose to give back to your community inspired me so many years ago. As I have completed higher education, I realize that people like you are rare. As black people rise in socioeconomic status and line the halls of academia, we begin to lose the connection we've had to ourselves as a people.

There is no community, no commonality between the black doctor and the black tradesman. Indeed, in law school I was disgusted at times at the lack of social consciousness and even the callousness of my contemporaries. Few seem to be interested in reaching back and touching the lives of the people who might need us. (And I don't just mean pro bono work, we don't serve as mentors, we don't volunteer yet we have time to plan lavish parties.) I cannot see the "talented tenth" reaching out into the community and helping others. Although that's not true across the board, I believe my generation could do more but has chosen to chase a materialistic dream and ignore the reality that is the destruction of our people.

Through all this, I have found wonderful people like you who have challenged and inspired me. I wanted to let you know that I took great notice of the work you have done and it has truly touched my life. I'm currently looking for a job and my schedule is very irregular because of it, but when I do acquire employment, I plan to resume volunteering. In the past I've worked with homeless children and children in state's custody and I find that it helps me to remain centered on the things that are truly important in life. You have taught me that it doesn't take great wealth to make a difference, only commitment. I thought it was important to let you know that you have created a legacy for young African Americans and I will always be touched by your generosity. Thank you so much for what you have done and what you continue to do in our community. I hope that one day I may indeed repay my debt by volunteering my time to your organization.

With Deepest Admiration,
Shani Franklin
Jurist Doctorate
University of Georgia- School of Law

As I read Shani's letter, tears welled up in my eyes, because before her letter there was never time to look back, all the way to the beginning. We had jumped from challenge to challenge, without taking the time to really assess our progress. Of course, there were many thank-you's along the way, but they were instant at-the-moment slices of appreciation - heartfelt and genuine, but for one deed at a time. Shani's letter somehow managed to encapsulate it all, and gift wrap it for me. And it went beyond any other recognition or award I had ever received for the entire community initiative. It was totally unexpected, and I was totally unprepared for it, because I had not gotten into this for adulation and celebrity. The irony was not lost on me, though, that when the recognition finally came, it was from corporations like Atlanta Mart and Turner Broadcasting System, and organizations like Georgia Center for Non-Profits. Secretly, I wondered where were *our* corporations, agencies and organizations. It wasn't like MKN was doing our thing underground. Our training program in the DeKalb Library, for example, brought the agency two Bill Gates (Microsoft) grants totalling $150,000 in 1999. They should re-name the Hairston Crossing Branch of the library after MKN, as far as I'm concerned. Thanks to the grant money they received, for MKN's Seniors Computer Workshop, the library was able to upgrade 23 branches of the library with new computer and presentation equipment that they didn't have before we came along.

Shani's letter was the note of appreciation that I never received from a grateful black community. I read it over and over again, because I knew that it had captured the essence of what I had envisioned for my contribution.

This letter capped a neighborhood initiative, PCs to the People, that promoted computer literacy in the underserved communities of south DeKalb County, Georgia. Whenever I retrace my steps towards community activism, the statistics are the most compelling reason

I found to get involved and do something. White households were noted as being twice as likely as blacks to own a computer. And even at income levels beyond $75,000, black households lagged far behind whites. The stats regarding black youth were even more alarming - fewer than one-third of black students owned a computer, in comparison to almost three-quarters of white students. The challenge was then clearly defined. I had to somehow try to change the perception and priorities of blacks, with regard to computers. Further, I had to develop a low cost method of promoting computer literacy to every age level – from school children to senior citizens.

The next step was to apply to the Internal Revenue Service for 501(c)3 non profit status. I did not have a clue as to how to apply, so I purchased a book and inquired with the Small Business Administration, which put me in contact with a person who walked me through the process by e-mail. Even with all of that help, however, the process was an extended journey through bureaucracy, with forms and requirements, the likes of which almost discouraged me. But through it all, I kept remembering those Digital Divide statistics.

Finally, when the notification of approval was received from the IRS, I started creating a strategy to make our presence known in the community. Mr. Kenyada's Neighborhood, Inc. was a legitimate non-profit organization, ready to get busy. Our website started to take shape, with a discussion board created by noted website designer, Robert Harris. People who I had met on the Internet started stepping into developmental roles. Glenn Hearn, Darni Bolden, Renee King, and good friend, Clara DeLay formed the think-tank nucleus of trusted MKN members. Darni got in touch with several high schools in the black community, announcing an essay contest, opened to students in those schools. The subject was about the importance of computer technology to African Americans. All students, regardless of race, were invited to enter, with the understanding that the subject matter would always be about blacks and computers. I think the students understood the point of this contest was really to get everyone onboard the technology superhighway.

We would present a brand new computer to the Grand Prize winner of the essay contest. I had no idea where I'd get the money for the prizes, but I knew we could not let a little detail like that stop the momentum.

I was worried, and despite the help, I felt that my inexperience with fund raising might kill this initiative before it really began.

My wife, Tricia, and I were invited to a restaurant. I didn't want to go, but Tricia insisted that I needed to get away from the pressure for a moment, so I agreed to go. We arrived at Youngblood's Restaurant in downtown Atlanta and, as we walked to the back of the place, I saw a few dozen people seated at tables - and they were all looking at me. "SURPRISE!" All of the people were members of the discussion forum on the website, including "Myster E," who flew in from Chicago. Most I had never met except for the Internet connection. They all came carrying donations in support of MKN's computer initiative. It was a wonderful night, and it was the last day I would feel alone in the Struggle.

While the essay contest was in development, I launched a five-year plan for a computer initiative I named "PCs to the People," to paraphrase the late Stokely Carmichael's 1960's clenched-fist call for "Power to the People!" Forty years later, we understood that access to personal computers (PC's) translated to education and knowledge. Knowledge is Power! In the 21st Century, we no longer ask for power, and our fists are clenched around a mouse and a keyboard. PCs to the People! This program would be the umbrella for all of our work to promote computer literacy in our community. We targeted three different groups of African Americans – children, teens (K-12), and seniors over 50. We began by launching the South DeKalb High School Essay Contest for the students in 11 predominately African American schools. For three consecutive years, MKN promoted computer technology by setting the themes of the essays to explore the importance of computers to the future advancement of blacks in America. Even with our main focus being on the computer advancement of our children, we could not forget our commitment to the entire community. From the very beginning, MKN understood the need to leave no one behind in the mad rush along the information superhighway. In 1999, SeniorNet, the recognized national leader in computer training for seniors, had but two locations in the metro area – one in Tucker, one off Northside Drive in Atlanta. There were no computer training facilities for seniors in the South DeKalb area. At that time, even the DeKalb County Public Library (DCPL) had no formal computer training schedule.

After speaking with many African American seniors about their concerns and reservations about computer technology, I wrote to the Director of the DCPL, Darro Wiley. I asked him if MKN could launch a computer training program for seniors, using the Library's facility, on Saturday mornings when the facility was closed to the general public. Wiley's response was very positive. He set up a meeting with MKN and Library administrators. When I and MKN Vice President Glenn Hearn met with the Library officials, we were prepared. I had outlined a proposed curriculum, as well as the results of research I had done into the funding available for such training.

People have asked me over the years how I started, what I did first. Since I was new to organizing, I figured i should make some sort of guideline for myself, perhaps even a code of ethics. I sat down at my kitchen table, with pad and pen, and I wrote out the following principles in less than 15 minutes.

MKN Core Values

We will always strive to promote self-respect, self-reliance and self-determination within the African American community.

The alliances we form with corporations and other community organizations will be based on the mutual understanding and acceptance of common goals to improve the lot of African Americans and, therefore, society as a whole.

We will always endeavor to go beyond the mere discovery and articulation of problems within the African American community, to seek out viable solutions to those problems.

We will be honest and trustworthy in establishing the methods, tactics and procedures with which to accomplish our goals.

We will continue to pay homage to our forebears, never forgetting the debt we owe to the African warrior, his King and his Queen.

We will not fight fire with fire. We will fight fire with water - to build rather than destroy; to listen as intently and purposefully as we speak.

We will strive to find an accord with our foes because we are a spiritual people who understand the strength of compromise. But lest those adversaries mistake our peaceful commitment, let them understand that integrity and determination are not the parentage of weakness.

We will promote computer literacy in the African American community, and increase the percentage of African American access to the Internet in order to strengthen our people's ascension into the 21st Century

In 2001, MKN and our PCs to the People program won two prestigious community service awards. The TBS Superstation Super 17 Award (in the Education category), and the overall Grand Prize of $20,000 went to MKN. Later that same year, I was awarded the Georgia Center for Nonprofits 2001 Above & Beyond Award.

Prison: Slavery, Part 2

One in nine black men between the ages of 20 and 34 is in prison. Some are calling the nation's prison system Slavery Part 2, and there are certainly enough black men in prison to make it qualify. There are other parallels, as well. Slavery was all about money, the Almighty Dollar. It meant cheap labor and huge profit margins for the southern states, just as the profits made through cheap prison labor today benefit those states with the largest prison populations.

Young black men are caught up in a judicial revolving glass door that cycles through poverty, ignorance, violence, criminality and incarceration. Rehabilitation is not even mentioned as part of the solution anymore. When we hear the word rehabilitation these days, it's usually about someone fixing up an old house. This is a national disgrace. We are a nation that recycles its cardboard, but throws away its people. Where is the incentive for prisons to rehabilitate its inmates when they are part of a free workforce of generally able-bodied men? Remember, the South would never have freed its slaves if left to their own devices. U.S. prisons, many of them privately-owned, have no intention of shutting down the cash register. It will be up to us to put an end to their supply of beasts of burden, but it will be difficult.

Many states groom young black men from school age, with police patrolling the hallways at school, keeping an eye out for potential "scholarships" to local jail cells. From that point, the new American slave trade takes on an official demeanor, with suits and civility. We see judges sitting up there on the auction block, handing out sentences like a closeout sale at Macys. If prison is not slavery, it's the closest we've come to it in a long, long time.

Of course, many would argue that the 13th Amendment of the United States Constitution, ratified in 1865, abolished slavery in the U.S. But let's take a closer look at that amendment as it is written:

13th Amendment, Section 1. Neither slavery nor involuntary servitude, except as a punishment for crime whereof the party shall have been duly convicted, shall exist within the United States, or any place subject to their jurisdiction.

"… except as a punishment for crime whereof the party shall have been duly convicted…" So slavery is still constitutional under certain circumstances, and what we are witnessing today can accurately be compared to classic slavery… with one possible exception – many of the black men in prison today were not forced to commit their crimes.

One in nine black men, ages 20-34, is in prison. One would think that over the years, we'd make progress with reducing those numbers, if only through attrition. But not when we've got knucklehead gangsta wannabees waiting in line for their golden opportunity to join the ranks of the incarcerated.

Young Black man, you could be practicing law, or practicing medicine. Instead you are practicing to become a career criminal - a gangsta, or Iceberg Slim, legendary pimp extraordinaire. Heed this warning: Black career criminals spend much more time incarcerated than working at their chosen career.

My Brother, all the resources of the entire U.S. Justice System are geared up for you. If they snare a few white guys along the way, it's just practice, while waiting for you. Every criminal law legislated; every police bullet fabricated was produced with you in mind. There was a time, not too long ago, when all the targets at shooting ranges of all the police academies in the country consisted of black humanoid figures holding guns. They can't build prisons fast enough for you, Black Man. Legislators cannot seem to find the funding for a new school, but they will transport your black ass to a brand new prison before the concrete is dry. Right now, somewhere in this country, they are building a jail cell with your name on it. The white contractor constructing the bars is so eager with anticipation that he can hardly contain himself.

Despite the literary title, Black men have never been invisible. White folks may act like they don't notice you, but you will never sneak up on them. We can't sneak anywhere; we can't hide anywhere. So if your plan is to make one big score and settle down in suburbia... forget it. They've got dogs trained to smell your blackness under a Brooks Brothers suit. So you know they'll sniff out your ass in a plaid shirt and Dockers. You are the most heavily sought after potential criminal on the face of the Earth. Every security camera moves at random, until it spots you, Black Man, and then you become its movie of the week. If you've ever wondered why so many stupid black criminals get caught on cameras, it's because it's an accident when a black man is *not* on a security tape.

They are coming after you, Black man. YOU; not your neighbor down the street (they'll get him later). And they'd like nothing better than to add you to their prison inventory as a low-paid inmate. In prison, like on the plantation, you will produce whatever needs to be produced – from clothing and furniture, to dormitory items and varied services. If there is a flood somewhere, you'll be sandbagging. If there is a fire somewhere, you'll be in the thick of it. They make money with your labor, and they make money when they overcharge you in the prison stores and the long distance phone fees. As an inmate you are a cash cow than can be shipped wherever you are needed to relieve overcrowding in local prisons.

We know that the U.S. Justice System is a loaded gun and a stacked deck, yet we continue to play the game, and act surprised when we lose. Maybe we should market incarceration as what it is - modern day slavery. Many young black men mistake prison as a rite of passage; something that makes them men. A Black man in chains was how this chapter in our lives began. But The African did not seek the chains, or run with deliberate speed onto those slave ships expecting a luxury cruise.

Preaching to the Choir

Years ago, we were all having an Internet discussion about race, black rage and white privilege. Computer keyboards were warming to the task, and the heat reached us all. Simone had not said a word, but a moment later we would all know that the pressure cooker had exploded. She addressed the African American nation, and no holds were barred.

Simone: *Needless to say, I've been reading with great interest - but the things happening with me right now are putting me into even MORE of a rage - a blind, hot rage - than usual. I can't even clearly articulate right now my feelings on race, inter- or intra-racial relations, and our need to act like crabs in a bucket - can't let one get to the top without getting pulled down by the others. As a people, we're such cheap and easy dates - anybody could take us anytime. We haven't mastered the art of big-picture and don't want to. We remain steeped in petty little adventures that don't speak to the future and the more global need. We answer to folks who don't have our best interests at heart, and sell out at the drop of a hat. We see it in our financial education, our need to buy that couch or Tahoe right NOW, our gratitude to those who fund us, and the way we raise our children. We take compliments as validation, and continue to seek validation from others because we still hate ourselves. We'll STILL pick the white doll.*

I'm glad that Simone said what needed to be said, and I'm happy that our forum was there to capture this enraged plea, really, to black folks. Of course, we all felt Simone's frustration and agreed with every point she made, but in agreeing, I began to understand something about those of us who stand up and make such comments.

On some levels, I suppose, it can be aptly described as "preaching to the choir," like-minded individuals who already understand and concur. The Choir already "believes." But I think what Simone and the rest of us understand is that all believers are not created equal. They are not all motivated or compelled to actually move, beyond mere belief, to implement Change. Nowadays many people use "Change" as a noun, that part of speech that is a thing. Barack Obama launched an entire presidential campaign on "Change" – the idea being that he alone represented Change and his opponents did not. Presidential candidates must campaign with wide paintbrushes for making the broad-brush strokes that paint a bright horizon.

The truth is that Change doesn't happen without change (small "c"), which is a verb - an action word. There are hundreds of thousands of people working at the grassroots level every day to make Change a reality. There are also thousands of people working to ensure that we fail… and some of those people are black, which was the point of Simone's comments. It would be great if those who need to hear this message were in the audience, but something tells me that they won't see it unless it appears in the local sports pages… or a comic book.

The good news about Simone's State-of-the-Black-Union is that it is within our ability to change it for the better. The most difficult aspect of the solution is that it requires a psychological re-mapping of something that was bred into black folk generations ago. It is, quite simply, that old you-ain't-shit theory of hopelessness that was handed down from generation to generation of under-achievers. It was usually proclaimed immediately after the consumption of liquor or drugs. And hearing such comments for the first time, the recipient was either stunned or stupefied, but never indifferent.

We need to continue to preach to the choir, particularly if it means that someone may be compelled to step up to the challenge. We've had more than our share of heroes and martyrs, who slew the dragons sent to destroy us. What we need now are black folk who understand that our toughest opponent will always be the enemy within ourselves. And it's never a bad idea to begin with the choir.

"Ya-know-what-i-mean?"

No, it's not "Do you know what I mean?" It's "Yaknowhatimean?"

And it's no longer a question (if it ever was). It's now a form of punctuation that young people use when they run out of vocabulary. "Yaknowwhatimean" is a comma, usually followed by a continuation of the same nonsense that preceded it.

Tommy doesn't spell well because he doesn't know any words. And Tommy doesn't know any words because he doesn't read anything deeper than the sports page or the liner notes on Snoop Dogg's latest CD.

"Yaknowhatimean?"

Challenge them. Stop them at mid-sentence and tell them that - HELL NO - you don't know what they mean. "Please explain it to me." Make them conscious of the phrase by letting them know that it's not acceptable. Insist that they speak in slower cadence, opening their mouths wide enough to give their tongues a chance to do a job, and their lips a chance to form consonants.

It's almost a cop out to blame parents and teachers, because they're fighting an uphill battle. Why stop there? Blame Wayan Brothers movies and Def Comedy Jam. Blame every black comedian who promotes Black 'n Stupid as an attribute. Place some of that blame on politicians and civic leaders who seem to endorse an acceptable level of failure for our youth. Blame the Black Church, too busy building monuments to moral mediocrity to challenge our youth with goals of scholastic excellence.

There seems to be no communication skill set promoted for, or by, our youth. It's a sobering thought to know that most of our kids would never catch a communicable disease if they actually had to communicate in order to catch it.

"Yaknowhatimean?"

The N Word – An Internet Discussion

Kevin: I would like to discuss the usage of the word 'nigga' by Black people in reference to each other. In my opinion, this is the biggest crime that we as Black people can perpetrate upon ourselves. This word was put on us by an ignorant, racist society many years ago. Yet here we are, in the 21st Century and this word still flows from our mouths. I've heard some say that when we say it, it's not used in a negative way. My question is...why would we want to use it period!

Phrases like..."that nigga's crazy" or "that's my nigga" have been spoken for many years...flowing from our mouths like a stagnant stream. Why do we continue to use this word? I know that old habits die hard...after all...isn't this just a bad habit? But isn't it time to change our habits? I don't care what the Webster's definition is...when people hear the dreaded 'n' word, they immediately associate it with Black people...a negative association at that! To top it off,our young people are carrying this torch, thus keeping 'nigga' alive and kicking. When you listen to 'some' rap music, not only do you hear the 'n' word, but you also hear women being referred to as 'bitches' and 'ho's'.

WAKE UP PEOPLE... Let this word go...forever! Don't get me wrong, when I was young, I too used this word. Everybody else was doing it...I thought it was 'cool'. But around my mid 20's, I'm 39 now, I started to examine

myself and what I was doing. Guess what? The 'n' word magically disappeared from my vocabulary. I promised myself that I would never refer to any Black person as a 'nigga' again. And I'm happy to say that I've kept that promise...never slipping, not even once. Tell the youth, show them by your example. Sometimes we as Black people can be our own worst enemies. We wonder why we are perceived in a negative light, yet we do the very things that perpetuate false stereotypes. What greater way to display self hate, than to call each other 'niggas'. Yes, we can say that when we use it, we're not doing it in a racially demeaning way. But the word itself denotes racism.

There is absolutely nothing good about the 'n' word... nothing! What must other ethnic groups think when they hear us use this word? I cannot tell you how many times people have asked me why Blacks call each other 'nigga'. Do Asians call each other 'chinks'? Do Latinos call each other 'wetback'? Even Africans wonder why we American Blacks do this. The time is now my brothers and sisters... we can be the masters of our own fate. We have made many positive strides, but we have a long way to go. The time is now to let the 'n' word go... forever!

Kenyada: You make very, very good points, My Brother, but may I suggest that you are preaching to a congregation already converted. I don't use the word, and I doubt that many at this level of black consciousness do. The challenge is to convince those who use it everyday, in every way – from a friendly greeting, to a part of speech or a point of punctuation.

We can stand on a street corner and shout at the top of our collective lungs, like the closing credits of a Spike Lee movie... but until we find some way to bridge the ever-widening gap between those of us who understand, and those who don't ... we will Never put the N-word (and every ugly synonym for it) to rest. We may, in time, remove it from our lyrics, strike in from polite conversation.... but can we ever cleanse its stench from our minds? By the way, it doesn't matter how you spell it – nigger or nigga – it's still the same disgusting word. There is no cleaning it up for a hip-hop audience.

Kalonji: Long ago I also used the "N" word, but only in the company of fellow African Americans. I felt that peer pressure was no excuse! That word denotes negativity! I stopped using it! I think it is a matter of knowledge.

During the twelve years of Eurocentric, brainwash, schooling, in this country's public education system; I was hungry for truth and it has only been within the last five years that I was able to allot time and money to get the truth! The truth about African history! The truth about World history! Once we learn about our glorious past! Once we learn of the many times we've fought back to foreign invaders! Once we learn of the tremendous contributions we builders of the Pyramids have made to this planet... then we will no longer use the "N" word! I recommend the following reading material as a start for all people on this earth to learn true history, but most especially for all African Americans!

Kenyada: I think your argument proves my point, and that is that if no white person ever uses that word again - it doesn't matter... because, as your point of view seems to indicate, we're on Automatic Pilot now. We have taken on the subliminal persona of our antagonists. We murder each with reckless abandon, we steal from each other ....we have devalued ourselves to the extent that there is no act of violence or self-hatred that we will not perpetrate on each other.

And we have adopted a word that evolved from the white southerner's inability to pronounce certain consonants and vowels correctly. "Negro," thus became "Nigra"...and the laziness of this particular speech impediment, allowed the "GRA" to be corrupted to "GA". And now we have made it our own; using it as a term of endearment.

To quote the persona that I take on whenever I hear it: "I pity the fool" - black, white or Martian- who calls me by that word. Age has nothing to do with it; it's about self-respect and respect for the memory of those who fought and died for their dignity; our dignity.

John: I see your point, and I really don't use the word that often. But, can we ignore the fact that using the word amongst ourselves takes the sting out of the word. I remember the first time I was called "Nigger" by a white kid. We were riding a school bus home. I was 10 years old; he was 15. I remember he hit me in the stomach at the same time. His punch didn't hurt, as a matter of fact, he started to cower because he knew I could come back and flatten his ass. But, you know what, I didn't, I couldn't. I was so disarmed and so completely embarrassed in front of my friends that all I could do was cry. I don't think he realized how that word is the "nuclear weapon" of insults, or maybe he did, and he knew that we'd be going to total war soon. In any case, now that word no longer has nearly the same impact.

Although, I don't like white people using it, I won't get nearly the same internal response to it, and I am able to punish the user more effectively.

Personally, I believe it is due to the desensitization I've built up to the word. It's no longer one of those taboo words that contain so much power. I think there is power in taking the weapons of your oppressor, and I believe that's what we've done by using the word ourselves.

Kenyada: It's interesting that you don't think that the white kid knew the power of the N-word. White people understand it more than you realize. In fact, they use the word as a tool to put you in your place. They use it like Lex Luther used Kryptonite to weaken Superman.

As for your "taking the weapons of our oppressor" argument... that logic would have us remove a gun from our oppressor's hand, and shoot ourselves in the head with it.

Nothing - not time, nor legislation; not repeating it every minute, of every day for the rest of your life - nothing will ever take the sting out of that word. And that is as it should be. Why? Because it is more than a word.... it is a festering sore in the catacombs of the African-American psyche.

You once said that you don't think about the lynching and other atrocities perpetrated against our people when you hear that word. Well, maybe you should. Maybe you should revisit those old documentaries wherein the bodies of black men were chained to tree trunks, castrated and burned, with the word Nigger hung around their necks. Think about it; and then think about what we are saying about ourselves when we use that term in OUR everyday conversation.

You are better than this, John. I've read your posts; you have an extraordinary command of the English language. You don't need that word. One more thing...

Fannie Lou Hamer

Malcolm X
Marcus Garvey
Jackie Robinson
Sojourner Truth
Arthur Ashe

Finally, ask yourself if the preceding is a list of Niggers ... or African-Americans deserving of far more respect that the word implies.

OLD SCHOOL JOURNEY

"Who are we as a people that we would allow another people to put a 28-day freshness date on our history and call it progress?"

Richad Kenyada

A Change is Gonna Come

One of the most meaningful songs ever recorded is Sam Cooke's "A Change is Gonna Come." It is haunting and lyrical, hopeful, yet sorrowful. In 1964, less than a year after Dr. King's historic "I Have a Dream" speech, Sam Cooke wrote an anthem for Change in this country. It was as much an affirmation as it was an assurance. When I heard it as a 17-year old boy, I didn't fully appreciate it for its simplicity. Most of the message songs of the 1960s hit you hard between the eyes with a sense of urgency and finality. It beat at its chest with volume, as if there were other answer and no other question worth answering.

I've often heard the song at varying stages in my adulthood, and the older I get the more I realize that the Change isn't necessarily about outside forces - natural or man-made - but rather the evolution within ourselves. Mr. Cooke alluded, throughout his lyrics, to racism and the effect it has in and on our daily lives. As a young man, I imagined that he meant that America would change, the white man ("I go to my brother, and I say, 'brother help me please.' But he winds up knockin' me back down on my knees"), the white racist would eventually change, and the institution of racism would erode and implode by the weight of its own wretchedness. But now I am convinced that the Change is something that each of us will encounter personally... if we are lucky.

For me, the Change was the point at which I began to understand and appreciate who I was and what my role would be in bettering the conditions that affect my people. It was also the juncture at which I accepted the challenge and was compelled to step forward. I didn't know at the time the significance of the Change. I just figured that it was a natural progression - you see a wrong, and you must correct it. You experience an injustice and you must fight back. And it's not because you feel that you can stem the tide of oppression alone. Your attitude is that if the levee breaks, I'll be damn if it breaks on my watch, in my sector. That's who I am, who I was raised to be, and I didn't know it before I was challenged to do something. The challenge welled up from within until it moved me. I could have run in the other direction, but the Change narrows one's options. It's no longer a multiple choice answer. You stand up, and you step forward.

When I pass on, someone who probably never even knew me will write words to define who I was, based on a thumbnail chronology that

104

captures the high points. There will be a short list of accomplishments and a shorter list of people who remember that I ever passed this way. It doesn't matter. When that time comes, I will have completed my mission... and that is to do what ever I could do, and accept that which was beyond my grasp. And I will leave confident that somehow, someway, sometime - for each and every one of us - a Change is gonna come. **Oh yes it will.**

Remembering Sister Rosa

Pssst! It's OK now; it's safe!

The lions, tigers, bears, Republicans, and other slimy things have gone back into their caves. The monsters back into the swamp; the vultures have ceased to circle Detroit. Rosa Parks has been carried to her final resting place, and we need no longer be concerned for her safety.

While watching the nationwide memorials for Mrs. Parks, I couldn't help but cringe each time I saw President Bush float Rosa Parks accolades like he was floating a loan. Maybe he was. After all, he was still trying to recover from the exposure of his race card, Hurricane Katrina.

Rosa Parks was one of the most courageous women in history. She will be remembered - in good company - with the likes of Sojourner Truth, Harriet Tubman, and Fannie Lou Hamer. When Mrs. Parks refused to get up and give her seat to a white man, whites didn't know what to think of her, and even some black people thought she was crazy. They rationalized that maybe, after a hard day's work, the woman was just too tired. But, as Sister Rosa remembered, in an interview, "The only tired I was, was tired of giving in… I knew somebody had to make the first step and I made up my mind not to move." It was remembered as an act of defiance. I'm sorry… an act of defiance? …for a black person in 1955? …for a black woman in 1955? …in Montgomery Alabama? An act of defiance was to EXHALE! What Rosa Parks did was to stare down an entire city of white people at a time when blacks didn't even know the color of white folks' eyes, having never lifted their own eyes above ground level. It's rather easy for some, to look back, secure in 2008 attitude, and believe that anyone could have accomplished Mrs. Parks' feat, but my point is that the strength and bravery of this beautiful woman contributed directly to the resilience of our entire race.

When asked what she thought would be the legacy of the civil rights movement, she responded that it was her hope that "memories of our lives, of our works and our deeds will continue in others." We honor Sister Rosa's memory when we rededicate ourselves to the ideals of freedom and equality that she held so dearly.

George W. Bush and his family are symbolic of the old South and the plantation mentality. He is the driver of that old Montgomery bus, steering us backwards, through anti-black Supreme Court nominees. Steering us backwards, through the second-class citizenry of New Orleans during Katrina. He was elected to alter our path toward freedom and equality, and he is the architect of the plan, the driver of the bus.

But like Rosa Parks, we don't have to stand for it.

Martin was a Man

Maybe this will be the year that I'll throw something at my TV set when that hair sprayed news anchor goes into his spiel about Martin Luther King, Jr's "dream." I am so tired of hearing sound bytes of media-selected speeches, particularly the "I Have A Dream" speech from the March on Washington. Invariably, we hear about the dream, but the content of the first half of the speech has been edited out. On the steps at the Lincoln Memorial in Washington D.C., Dr. King told the world, "...we have come to our nation's capital to cash a check ...a promissory note to which every American was to fall heir. This note was a promise that all men would be guaranteed the inalienable rights of life, liberty, and the pursuit of happiness. It is obvious today that America has defaulted on this promissory note insofar as her citizens of color are concerned." Those observations are not the sedate, idle ramblings of a dreamer. Martin was a Man. He told the truth, and he related his vision for the future, but that's not the way historians are playing it back. Once a year we get a capsule-version of Martin: Like America is saying, "take two of these and call me after King Day." Please don't misunderstand. I admired and respected this man in Life, just as I revere him in death, but I'm convinced that the media, perhaps even America, doesn't get it. Martin Luther King, Jr. had a vision, but he wasn't a dreamer.

I have searched the World Wide Web, various magazines and film documentaries for a photograph of Martin actually dreaming. No luck. All I can find is Martin the father; Martin the husband; Martin the Freedom Fighter; the Nobel Peace Prizewinner; the man of God. Martin the put-upon, bone-weary icon. But not one dreamer in the bunch. "Dreamer"? Maybe it was a little civil-rights-leader hype. Perhaps Dr. King told us his vision was a dream to mercifully put it into a context that mere mortals could comprehend. Sometimes great leaders do that for their followers; giving them the Readers Digest version so as not to confuse them.

Martin was an ordinary man blessed with the wisdom, strength and sense of purpose that compelled him to do extraordinary things. Had he been a dreamer - dreaming as much as the media now credits him with - it is doubtful that he would have accomplished as much as he did. He was too busy to dream. He believed in the power of faith, but he also believed in the ethic of hard work. It is his vision that carried him forward. It is his vision that supplied the road map to his greatness.

Another misconception we hear a lot at this time of year is the term "Civil Rights March." Martin Luther King, Jr. never marched. Marching is what the Florida A&M Band does so well. Martin walked, which is a tougher mile without the musical accompaniment. Martin walked long, hard miles - singing, arm-in-arm miles. Hot, humid miles. You don't march across summer's molten Mississippi asphalt with any extended sense of cadence. You walk... gingerly. Martin walked those look-over-your-shoulder-for-a-sniper miles in the South. But he also walked the racist streets of Cicero, Illinois and, for the uninformed, those were dodging-rocks-and-spit miles. That he could continue to move forward against such a formidable foe, is a true testimony to his greatness.

So this year, as we celebrate Dr. King's birthday, let us honor Dr. King as Man, not dreamer or deity. The Dream has been given more power than it deserves. In his all too brief life on this Earth, Martin stood proud and erect, with his feet firmly planted in reality. While the media would have us believe that the sum total of his life rests in the words of a single speech, we somehow must move beyond the words and live our lives with his vision intrinsically woven to our own.

Frank Wills:
America 's Night Watchman

I was born on June 17, 1947. Prior to that year, the day was noteworthy for the 1775 Battle of Bunker Hill in which the British won the battle with the highest casualties (800) of any battle in the Revolutionary War. But I digress. Twenty-five years after I was born - on June 17, 1972 - the break-in of the Watergate office complex in Washington D.C. changed the course of history. Enter brother Frank Wills.

Twenty-four year old Frank Wills, a native of Savannah, Georgia visited Washington D.C. in 1971 and liked it so much he decided to stay. Later that year, a security services firm hired Frank to work as an $80-a-week security watchman on the midnight-to-7 a.m. shift at the Watergate office complex.

Early morning, about 1 a.m. on June 17th, on one of his rounds, Wills noticed a piece of tape covering the lock mechanism on a door between the basement stairwell and the parking garage. Frank didn't immediately see any great significance in the tape. He removed it and continued his rounds. About an hour later, Frank Wills again made his rounds, and discovered that the same door had been re-taped.

Brother Wills then called the D.C. police, and the rest is history. The police arrested five men in the offices of the Democratic National Committee. Had it not been for the work of Frank Wills, that burglary may have gone unnoticed, giving the Republicans unlimited access to confidential Democratic information. Can one man change history? You bet he can! And his station in life doesn't really matter; at least it didn't in the case of Frank Wills. One man, working as a security guard, was the key player in bringing down the Nixon White House. His service on the night of June 17th resulted in the convictions of G. Gordon Liddy, James McCord, Charles Colson, John Ehrlichman, President Nixon's Chief of Staff, H.R. Halderman, and an alphabet soup of movers and shakers at 1600 Pennsylvania Avenue. Of course.

the most earth-shattering result of all was the resignation of President Richard M. Nixon.

"He's the only one in Watergate who did his job perfectly," said Washington Post reporter Bob Woodward, speaking of Frank Wills "...Calling the police was one of the most important phone calls in American history, and it was so simple and so basic."

Wills started receiving due recognition for his efforts as the importance of the night in history became more evident. The Democratic Party gave him an award. Civil Rights organization, the Southern Christian Leadership Council gave Wills the Martin Luther King Award. He was even cast to portray himself in "All The President's Men," the Robert Redford film about Watergate. But soon afterward, Brother Wills' celebrity had run its course. After a few talk show appearances, and half-baked attempts to capitalize on his name, Wills was reduced to a footnote in history, while several of the burglars went on to write books.

Frustrated over not receiving a raise for his heroics, Mr. Wills quit his job at the security firm the following year. But he never anticipated that he would have much trouble finding another job. He commented to the Washington Post: "I don't know if they are being told not to hire me, or are just afraid to hire me." Wills spent the next several years moving from job to job, occasionally scoring a few dollars on the talk show circuit, but the price he paid for those appearances was the loss of jobs due to the travel time required. He was arrested in 1983 for shoplifting a one-dollar pen and a $12 pair of sneakers.

Destitute and suffering from a brain tumor, Brother Wills moved in with his ailing mother and took care of her until she died two years later. He couldn't even afford to bury his mother, and had to donate her body to science. Afterwards, he remained in his mother's old house with no electricity or water.

In his latter years, Frank Wills rarely spoke of Watergate, and by the time of the 25th anniversary of Watergate,1997, Wills was a forgotten man, who had grown bitter and frustrated. In a Boston Globe interview, he said: "I put my life on the line. If it wasn't for me, Woodward and Bernstein would not have known anything about Watergate. This wasn't finding a dollar under a couch somewhere."

Frank Wills died penniless Wednesday, September 27, 2000, in a hospital in Augusta , Georgia . He was only 52.

June 17th, the day of my birth, in some way, intrinsically ties me to this important figure in American History. Each year I am taken back to that fateful early morning discovery of Mr. Wills, and I wonder why it is that decent men must always bear the burden of those of lesser worth. As we mourn the brother who simply did a job the way it was supposed to be done, let us know, beyond the telling of the story, that Frank Wills was indeed a hero. He did not give us everything, but he gave us all he had.

Somewhere in this great nation there should be a monument erected in honor of Frank Wills. Chiseled from the blackest Onyx, and made to stretch its strong ebony arm toward the heavens. If Justice can be a blindfolded white woman, Truth can be a Black man who served well as America's Night Watchman.

Rest in Peace, Brother Frank. Rest in Peace. We will carry on ...

The Next Level

I keep hoping that African America will abandon its so-called leaders, who are slowly dying off anyway, and chart a new course for The Next Level. There's no shame in admitting the error in our search for integration. It was merely a slight miscalculation, that's all. We thought that, as Americans, white folks would eventually get it and accept the fact that we are here to stay, so we -- all of us – would put aside the petty crap and get on with the building of a stronger nation.

We were wrong.

The roots of the entrenched, institutionalized, racism run much too deep to ever hope to eradicate it. And while there are many white American allies in our struggle for equality, the bottom line in this balance sheet will always be black.

It was once thought that racism would suffer the fate of a cleansing attrition, with the old line bigots dying out, and new, more enlightened offspring who are better educated, rising to champion diversity and equal opportunity.

We were wrong there, too.

Bigots beget bigots, and the better educated children of the 1960's and 70's racists have only changed their forebears' tactics, not their own minds. Their continuing challenge to affirmative action, for example, relies heavily on funding from the Rupert Murdock-type corporations rather than the quasi-racist organizations of the past. Meanwhile, African America spins its wheels appealing to the nation's sense of fair play, which has been somewhat strained since white males started losing interviews to better qualified, higher educated black women.

The Next Level will accept certain givens in American race relations. First of all, it will take whites out of the equation. This is not about them, it's about us. The longer we continue to make whites, and their acceptance of us, the focal point of any dialog regarding our advancement, we are doomed to stagnate and fail.

What we must do is concentrate our efforts, our resources and, yes, our prayers on the one determining factor in the liberation of African Americans.... African Americans. We are our best ally; we are our worst foe. We must form solid, community-based organizations specifically for the purpose of political, economic, and social advancement. We must recognize the value in each of us. Successful communities rely heavily on varying contributions – time, vocational skills, professional abilities. We all have something to contribute; we just may need someone to recognize what are our individual specialties.

The Next Level is rhetoric-free, hype-challenged, pro-active. The planning stages are over – been there, done that. The time for quiet reflection on the romanticism of the civil rights era has passed. There will be no more singing, and swinging, in the throes of the old civil rights songs. I can't stand one more stanza of "We Shall Overcome." I've eaten at the formally segregated southern dinettes, where 35-year old bloodstains still hide, deep in the dark seams of the Formica lunch counter. There they scream for retribution, unheard over the lip-smacking clamor for second helpings of pork biscuits. As white hands handed me a menu, I realized the irony in the war we waged. We fought for the right to sit on the wrong side of that counter, when we should have been fighting for the right to stand on the other side ...the side with the cash register. This is, after all, America.

The Next Level won't be particularly politically correct. We will come to the realization that we must cut our losses. We've run out of other cheeks to turn, in confronting an enemy that has become increasingly ....ourselves.

Why do we always have to be the moral conscience of this society? Why are we always expected to take the higher ground? When will we come to grips with the fact that the ground has become higher only by virtue of the fact that our expired bodies continue to be strewn across it? The challenge is ours, not Clinton's or Ted Turner's. Instead of marching to Washington, we'd better start marching into our children's rooms – not to talk, but to listen.

We'd better start offering our children a new vision of themselves, one that doesn't involve a basketball or a bassinet. If our children are not speaking the language of morality, we'd better learn a different language, one that will translate our support and guidance. We need to take some of that stock morality play we've been holding onto for centuries and re-invest it into our children. If we choose to teach them to pray, it had better be with their heads up and eyes open. We had better teach them more than the Nancy Reagan pipe dream of, "just-say-no." We had better teach them affirmation, saying "Yes" to something, as an alternative to saying "No" to everything. And that 'something' had better be themselves.

Yes, teach them about Jesus, but not the Jesus who felt sand between his toes; the Jesus who walked on solid ground. The Jesus who worked at keeping it real, ages before the term was ever coined. De-mystify your Prince to give Him meaning to our children, who desperately need to see a connection between Him and themselves. By moving to the next level of religious training, we give our children a part of themselves that many of them have never been in touch with. The spirituality that is strength, rather than passive; the spirituality that stands for something, rather than against everything. The Next Level will be more introspective than retrospective, more cerebral and life affirming than tactical and statistical. It will move us beyond the symbolism of the sixties and the blank-verse poetry-driven militancy of the seventies. The lessons learned since then center around what has not worked more than what has worked.

It has been said that the 21st century will be the Age of Data – the dissemination of it, the translation of it into information, and the analytical assessment of the information, which will filter it into a foundation of knowledge. Once that corner is turned, such knowledge becomes power, the great equalizer.

The Next Level awaits us. The question remains, are we capable of achieving it?

New Year, Same Old Me

We all use the term "New Year" as some sort of milepost, which it is. But the term also implies Change to many of us. Perhaps it's just wishful thinking, but we call such plans for Change "resolutions." We resolve to do better, lose weight, exercise, be kinder to our neighbors. Of course, the only problem with such plans is that they require action. Change for the New Year is not a passive spectator sport. It demands that we DO SOMETHING, and make at least a minimal commitment to get it done.

The one resolution I've ever made turns out not to have been a New Year's Resolution. Instead of January 1st, it was made on November 1st, 1975 – the day my son was born. I resolved to quit smoking cigarettes – from 2-packs-a-day down to zero packs a day. I looked at him in his hospital bassinet, and I promised us both that I had smoked my last KOOL; my last cigarette of any brand. There was no reservation, no wavering in my mind's voice – it was simply something that was done, period.

That was 32 years ago. I had buried my Dad 11 months earlier after he died from lung cancer. He was only 55 years old, a willing victim of decades of Camel and Phillip Morris cigarettes, but I continued to smoke, thinking (?) that I was invincible after surviving two tours of duty in Nam. In fact, even when I quit smoking, it wasn't to save myself; it was to spare my newborn son the uncomfort of what was then still theoretical, "second-hand smoke." Talk about the Power of Love! My kid saved my life before he enjoyed his first pee. New Year's Resolutions tether us to what we conceive to be our better selves – thinner, younger, kinder, smarter, richer. So we make these resolutions with the best of intentions in January, but begin to falter in February. I think I know why. An intention without a commitment is like a treasure map drawn in the sand. The slightest breeze will alter the outcome. But even an earnest commitment is not enough to ensure

113

success. The commitment needs more; it needs the passion to see it through. My success 32 years ago was fueled by my passion for the commitment to protect my son. Without passion, commitment is like an autumn leaf – you don't know where it came from, or where it's going. You just know that it's temporary.

We say "New Year" as if there is actually something new about it. Maybe it would be more accurate to call it Another Year, without the implied discovery of uncharted territory. I have always questioned the absurdity of placing such importance on the changing of the calendar. Will the New Year bring us something that we don't have already or just more of the same tired ass shit? Will there be any less killing or war? Any less racism or disease? We will draw the chronological line at the end of the year... and then continue with business as usual. The realist in me rejects the pomp and ceremony of The New Year, while the optimist in me stays invested in its promise - the promise of Hope.

Hope prevails; life finds a way. Donny Hathaway sang the lyric "...take it from me, someday we'll all be free"... and then he promptly took a header off his balcony. He only had a little bit of hope left, and it was – all of it - for us. Of course, there is nothing revolutionary about taking your own life. Suicide is surrender, going down voluntarily. If there is a more selfish act of cowardice for a black man, I cannot imagine what it could be. Each of us must find our own strength. For me, it is in the written word and the fire that it brings. I have to write because the tears aren't enough, and sometimes the scream won't come. I have to write, because walking in the right direction won't get me there. Writing, for me, is a response, but it's also a preemptive strike. I need to write, even at times when the words aren't there. Writing is my other voice, my inner voice. Most often, I speak out loud in a language that is, in some way, compromising – to convey understanding rather than questioning. It is void of the passion and real commitment that I feel.

I'm still waiting to mellow. They say it should have come by now. Maybe the New Year will bring it. I am over sixty - an age when I'm supposed to be settling in on senior citizenry. I'm supposed to be very accepting of the way things are, the status quo. Short of moving to Florida and patiently waiting for the inevitable – excess gas and a Bush brother screwing with my vote – I'm not supposed to be looking for answers anymore. I'm supposed to drive in the slow lane, and take my time on left turns, crossing on-coming traffic. Screw that! I'm taking my full swing, and planning on clearing the bases

I'm supposed to be going to church regularly and getting right with God. Singing songs, carrying my own hymnbook and Bible. But whom would I be trying to fool? God knows what he's got to deal with here. I was never one to perpetrate for a good seat at a Temptations concert, let alone standing room at the Pearly Gates. Something is wrong. I don't feel any of the things I thought I would feel at this age. I still feel like fighting. Granted, I'm in no condition to go the full 15 rounds, but I'm confident I can find the right moment for a knockout.

The AARP started sending me junk mail 13 years ago. I threw it in the trash. Looked up in the sky and they were circling like condors waiting for me to slow down. I have contempt for many of my contemporaries – desperate to be the kind of Old they saw in their grandfathers' eyes. I'm pissed. I can't even grow old like everyone else. I ain't going quietly into the night. I've got stuff to do and places to go, And when I die, it will probably be on my way to kicking someone's ass over something I should have let pass.

What New Years' do best is to reinforce hope. Maybe it is false hope, but at least false hope gives you a break in the madness. It ain't gonna cure anything, but it ain't gonna hurt anything either. For those of us who have lost faith, hope is the only thing we've got going. And the New Years allow us to gather the little hope we have left over and add it to a fresh supply promised by a brand new calendar.

James Brown

(December 25, 2006) I lost my soul today. James Brown died and I lost my soul. I've never known a day in my adult life that did not have soul, because James Brown was always there. Before Motown, there was James Brown. Before the the Memphis Sound, and the Philly Sound, there was James Brown. Before Hip-Hop there was James Brown. James Brown was always there in the background, providing the backbeat and, at times, the backbone, to African American music.

Say It Loud, I'm Black and I'm Proud
Don't Be a Dropout

Papa Don't Take No Mess

Whatever needed to be said, we could always count on James Brown to say it. He was the first leader of any kind to step forward and preach the gospel of ownership... the ownership of responsibility, as well as property. "I Don't Want Nobody to Give Me Nuthin' (Open Up the Door, and I'll Get it Myself). He was flawed and failing at times, but those imperfections seemed to endear him even more to the rest of us, because it allowed us to see the man succeed in the midst of his own problems.

In the 1960's, with record companies rushing to "clean up" black recording artists to be more accepted by white record buyers, James Brown remained true to his roots. His music remained funky when compared to Pat Boone, but even funkier when compared to Motown. Motown was busy plunking white couples on the covers of Isley Brothers albums, while James Brown was pictured in all his sweaty glory.

I remember him in Vietnam, where he visited twice during my two tours of duty. When Bob Hope came to the war zone, there was an unwritten code that many, many black troops were sent elsewhere so that the cameras would capture a mostly white military audience. But when James Brown came over, he told them that he wanted to see his audience full of black faces. Period. And you better believe that we were there in record numbers. His shows were magnificent! No one moved like James Brown. No one commanded the stage like he did.

His later missteps included the embracing of Richard Nixon and the Republicans, but that was only because of his insistence on black ownership and self-determination. They sold him a bill of goods, not unlike the bill of goods they sold to the Black Church in 2004.

James Brown will be remembered for many things, but it is his music that will always provide the backdrop for those images. The first record producer that produced a record on microphone, while it was being recorded... "Mr. Engineer, keep it going; we're gonna try sumthin' here..." That was Mr. Brown and his JB's creating, playing, editing and recording music on the spot.

He started out shining shoes and ended his life giving toys and food to the needy. In between all that, he made the most original music ever recorded. Peace, Brother James... Rest in Peace.

We'll open up the doors and get it ourselves.

Thanksgiving 2008

Just over three weeks ago, an African American named Barack Obama was elected President of the United States of America. Historically, Thanksgiving conjures up the retelling of the story of the original Thanksgiving feast of 1621 with the Pilgrims and Indians. But this most recent event clears the table, doesn't it? With the election of Barack Obama, America comes of age and steps through the pages of it own history to finally realize its promise. Obama's election was not only a barometer of this country's efforts to deal with its failings; it was the beginning of a new journey forward.

Forty-five years after the assassination of Dr. Martin Luther King, Jr., this nation has grown as much as it has changed. Immigration - both legal and illegal - has forced America to let out a few notches on its belt – much like we do at the table of a Thanksgiving feast. And like that first Thanksgiving feast, everyone is invited. For the first time in this country's history, everyone has a place at the table.

Black people have lived all over Washington D.C., with the exception of one specific piece of real estate – 1600 Pennsylvania Avenue. We have cooked there, cleaned there, stood guard there… but we have never lived there. Hopefully, on January 20, 2009, the Obama family, a black family will move into The White House, and later that year, we will all celebrate another First Thanksgiving.

And for that blessing, we will, indeed, be thankful.

15 Minutes

In 1968, pop culture icon Andy Warhol said, "In the future everyone will be world famous for 15 minutes." At the time, he was referring to the fleeting condition of celebrity that grabs onto an object of media focus, and then passes on to some new object as soon as the public's short attention span is exhausted. Things have changed.

In '68, Warhol's words were considered a sad commentary on the world of entertainment. But today, we are experiencing the "future" he predicted, with overnight celebrity status being bestowed upon even the least of us. Somehow performance has been replaced by hyperbole as the litmus test for celebrity.

In the old days people used to just sing in the shower, or pretend that their hairbrushes were microphones while they lip-synched in the mirror. Today those wannabes upload the hairbrush performance onto YouTube or MySpace. Instant 15 minutes of fame.

What's missing most, of course, is the work ethic. The idea that one must apply one's self, and study one's craft in order to succeed is missing in the instant oatmeal approach to entertainment. The legendary performers spent years perfecting their craft - learning comedic timing, voice training, stage presence, acting and improvisation. Then they found initial crumbs as street performers, or opening acts in small comedy clubs. They labored at carnivals and amusement parks – any place to be seen, as well as to learn. To think that a few moments on national TV or the Internet can catapult marginal talent to a status simply unknown to the real stars of yesteryear… that's insane.

Those of us in the audience, who have witnessed greatness on the stage, screen and television, have a basis for comparison and, while the cheap imitation for entertainment is amusing to some, no one is accepting it as the real thing. Missing are the standards. You can only appreciate fringe entertainment when you have a standard by which to measure it. So a talent show like The American Idol isn't necessarily the evil empire that purists make it out to be.

We had talent shows back in the day, such as Ted Mack's Original Amateur Hour, which is where a 7-year-old Gladys Knight won the contest in 1951. The difference is that we knew Ted Mack's Original Amateur Hour was no substitute for The Ed Sullivan Show, where show business legends performed. Ted Mack was the Mickey Rooney/ Judy Garland, "I've-got-a-trumpet-you've-got-a-barn-let's-put-on-a-show type of entertainment. But it was never mistaken as the standard bearer.

It all boils down to R-E-S-P-E-C-T. If an aspiring entertainer is going to excel in a profession – any profession – he or she must first respect the profession enough to study it. Study its history, and its pioneers. And it doesn't matter how long he's been in the business, the great ones never stop learning.

In the late 1960's, I attended an after-party for the great Sammy Davis Jr.'s opening night in Las Vegas. He was still pumped after the show, as he moved from guest to guest, meeting and greeting. But when he noticed Billy Eckstine enter the suite, Sammy ran over to him and guided him through the crowd to a comfy chair. He tossed a big pillow on the floor in front of Mr. Eckstine, who was one of the show business elder statesmen. Sammy sat down in front of him and could be overheard asking for Mr. Eckstine's opinion about the show and the song selection.

I could hardly believe my eyes. In a room full of entertainers, Sammy Davis, Jr. – pound-for-pound, the best entertainer on the planet, was playing a scene from Kung Fu, as Grasshopper to Billy Eckstine's Master Po. It was a moment that I'll never forget, because it demonstrated that greatness has no freshness date. It's an absolute – either you have it, or you don't.

And when you have it, 15 minutes is just another infomercial.

Thank You, Brother John H. Johnson

The first time I saw a magazine with a black person on its cover, I must have been about 6- or 7-years old. It was there, wedged in between the Look, Life, Newsweek and Time. It wasn't even a full cover. Many years later, my Dad told me that I pointed to it and he pulled it out. I smiled a smile of familiarity, like seeing a family member. The person on the cover – I don't readily recall if it was Jackie Robinson, Marion Anderson or Ralph Bunche – that person had black skin. And it was as if a door had opened for me. In that small world of mine, where every published image was white, every greeting card, every TV commercial, every newspaper ad – smiling white folks. It was Ebony Magazine, and it colorized my little world as much as it enlarged it.

When I heard of Publisher John H. Johnson's passing – in an 8-second blip on the evening news – I was deeply saddened. But then I smiled briefly as I realized the absurdity of the 20-minute clip of newsman Peter Jennings' passing next to the brief coverage of Johnson. Surely, Mr. Jennings would have been as incensed as he would have been embarrassed. But then I realized that this is why Ebony has always been there – to give us the full story, beyond the racist editors and assignment desks.

Ebony and Jet gave us something that we desperately needed… *ourselves.*

Rest in Peace, My Brother

WAR , DAP & THE BLOODS

"I'm a Vietnam Veteran, and I stand shoulder to shoulder with other Vets – the mentally ill ones, the homeless ones, the divorced and destitute, those dying from the effects of Agent Orange, and those dying from neglect in veteran's hospitals."

I Am a Veteran

For a Veteran, particularly one who has served in a combat zone, every day is Veteran's Day. It never leaves you. It's always there – just beneath the surface if you're lucky; on your sleeve, if you're not. In many ways, it defines who you are; it predicts what you will do.

Vietnam Veterans are a special breed, because Vietnam was the first war in which the United States was in denial. Our role was suspect, our motives were in question, and our morals were abandoned. It was not our grandfathers' war, fought in honor, for an honorable cause. It was not our fathers' war, fought without question or pause. Vietnam was a Family Dollar Store war, fought with bogus, no-name remnants of misplaced self-respect. We fought for a trumped-up cause that we had lost on paper long before we lost in the rice paddies of Vietnam.

America lost its cherry in Vietnam, but the Vietnam Vet lost his humanity. For many of us, it was impossible to return home as we had left. We came back disillusioned and gutted; empty in every respect that means anything. Even those of us who didn't feel we had lost anything, didn't realize we had lost the ability to feel. Walking around looking perfectly normal, but void inside. Making it back alive meant nothing, no thing. It was just another rouse; just another scene being played out for the audience of our friends and family. But we could not fool ourselves. At home, at night, in the darkness, our bodies ached with the loneliness of one hand... clapping.

The loneliness every veteran feels initially can sometimes compel him to seek shelter. I found my shelter in accepting my rightful place in the lineage of African American Veterans who had come before me. The healing process for me began when I became more aware of the contributions of other African American soldiers in other wars by studying the wealth of available information on these real-life heroes and she-roes. From the black recipients of the Congressional Medal of Honor, to the Buffalo Soldiers, who made Teddy Roosevelt look good in the Spanish-American War; to the Tuskegee Airman, who escorted bombers to and from targets during WW II, and never lost one. And I knew I had to also accept responsibility for their descendants. For me that responsibility meant becoming invested and involved with the cause of the Digital Divide, and the founding of Mr. Kenyada's

Neighborhood, a non-profit dedicated to the promotion of computer literacy.

I'm a Vietnam Veteran, and I stand shoulder to shoulder with other Vets – the mentally ill ones, the homeless ones, the divorced and destitute ones, those dying from the effects of Agent Orange, and those dying from neglect in veteran's hospitals. We shared something on those fields of combat that few can ever understand or relate to. It is something from which we can never be cured or medicated, something that will last for the rest of our lives. All that each of us has any right to expect is that the next Veteran, the next grunt in line, remembers one of us on Memorial Day and Veteran's Day.

EPILOGUE

Two Richard W. Harpers from New York – one white, the other Black - went to Vietnam in 1967, but only one returned home. U.S. Army Reservist, 1st Lieutenant Richard W. Harper was killed on January 31, 1968 in Gia Dinh, South Vietnam. He was a casualty of hostile ground fire and died from multiple fragmentation wounds. His body was recovered and returned home to Baldwin, New York. His name is engraved on Panel 36E, Line 12, on the Vietnam Veteran's Memorial Wall.

The other Richard W. Harper returned home to New York after serving two tours of duty in Nam. He knew nothing of his namesake until 1985 when he visited the traveling Vietnam Veterans Memorial Wall in downtown Atlanta. As he walked along the display looking for the name of a friend, he came upon his own former name – Richard W. Harper. And for one split second, it was almost as if he had not made it back home. He touched the engraved name, slowly tracing its outline with his fingers.

Perhaps it was at that moment that one Vietnam Veteran finally found the strength to let go of the past and move forward, once again thankful to be alive.

Wounded Soldiers: Wounded Again at Home

As a Vietnam veteran, I was deeply moved by the series of stories in The Washington Post last month that documented a variety of problems at Walter Reed Army Medical Center. There, veterans who lost limbs, and veterans with brain injuries, are living in moldy, rat-infested rooms that would make our worse prisons look like luxury suites. The so-called "Building 18," is a motel turned dormitory, because the Medical Center was overwhelmed by the real cost of the War in Iraq. The healthcare – or shall I say, the lack of healthcare – being received by these soldiers, is now being spotlighted by a House panel studying the newspaper stories. I'm encouraged, because I know that Walter Reed Army Medical Center has been just the tip of the iceberg. And if mold and rats are what our wounded soldiers must endure at a military hospital in the nation's Capitol, I dread the quality of the healthcare being provided in the other 11 military medical centers around the country.

I thought that America had hit rock bottom when Bush started shipping home the body bags under the cover of darkness, and forbidding photographs of the caskets. But I was wrong. It turns out that the plight of a wounded soldier in this country at times makes a body bag look appealing. I'm not sure that other Americans are ready to see the real cost of this war splashed nightly across their TV screens, but it's necessary. The wounded soldier has been, until this point, swept under the rug and hidden in the attic. And it makes this old veteran wonder what is worse – being killed in action, or being killed by neglect.

9/11 - 24/7

It's been seven years. Seven whole years. For me, that fact changes everything I had ever felt about man's relationship to Time, because it doesn't feel like seven years. It doesn't even feel like one year, for a New Yorker. It feels like one unyielding hour of horror running in slow motion on an endless loop. I've found that it doesn't matter your proximity to Ground Zero. If you are a New Yorker, there is no distance or measure or time that removes and insulates you from the 9/11 loss. They tell you to move on with your life, like you've just lost a basketball game. But the World Trade Center was a part of our home, and it will never be the same.

9/11 changed America, and it changed Americans. I know it changed me in ways I never before thought possible. I've been anti-religion for as long as I can remember, but since 9/11 I've become an unapologetic agnostic. I've always felt indifference with regard to the Middle East, but since 9/11, I emphatically want nothing to do with Muslims, and don't care too much either for Israel. I've come to accept religion as other people's heartfelt fiction, a concoction of words, images and imagination, created to blind us from truth and bind us with lies. No one in history has used religion to advance lies better than George W. Bush. Intellectually, I can understand how a no-dick butcher like George W. Bush could have succeeded in lying to the American people. But I know he was assisted by black people in the pulpits of our churches. I can never accept nor forgive the gullibility of African Americans who were duped by their own Christian beliefs into supporting The Bush Lie.

President Bush pimped 9/11 to support his digression into Iraq. Over 30,000 American soldiers have been wounded, and over 4,100 American soldiers have been killed in Iraq. And it seems that Bush is determined to see how many more he can kill. In his warped sense of retribution, Bush continues to use the increasing death toll as a reason to stay longer. He likens the voices calling for withdrawal to those who would have appeased the Nazi empire. What he doesn't seem to understand is that if a parallel is to be drawn from Nazi Germany, it is Bush who will come off as Adolph.

Everyone realizes that there was never any connection between 9/11 and Saddam Hussein. Duhhh!!! It was all done with George W. Bush smoke and mirrors. The Weapons of Mass Destruction were the smoke; the "War on Terror" quotes were the mirrors. And thus, a fraud was perpetrated on the American public. The War in Iraq is a distraction from the terror of 9/11, not a result. No one knows where Osama Bin Laden is, but my guess is that he's got a lot of hiding space in between the lies of George Bush. And every time Bush steps up his game plan to include muddying the line between Bin Laden terror and American aggression in Iraq, we should all gag in his face.

The Bush Family agenda for the invasion of Iraq goes all the way back to the original President George Bush. And for that reason, 9/11 is quite possibly the best thing that ever happened for the Bush Family. [How do ya like that, Barbara?] It gave Bush all the excuse he needed to invade Iraq, and connect the aggression to 9/11 payback. Had 9/11 not happened, Bush would have had to create another excuse for the invasion.

Seven years after 9/11, Bush continues to use the attack, but his house of cards has begun to crumble under the weight of his own bullshit. Dr. King said that a lie can't last forever. Former Bush Deputy Press Secretary Scott McClellan's memoir, "What Happened: Inside the Bush White House and Washington's Culture of Deception," exposed the Bush bullshit for what it is. And with this book, probably the first of several, The Big Lie has begun to unravel. It was McClellan's job to defend Bush's policies during much of the War in Iraq and the aftermath of Hurricane Katrina. But he now says the Bush Administration became an instrument of propaganda and political spin, and played loose with the truth in order to win the support of the American people. A pack of lies. The past 7 years have been a pack of presidential lies tied neatly with a bow of bullshit. But it seems that the bastard has run out of smoke and mirrors because the other rats are now jumping ship… with tell-all books as buoys.

As the toll of American soldiers killed or wounded in action continues to grow, the American people have lost their patience. The candidacy of Barack Obama continues to look like the only alternative to the Bush/McCain war strategy. So eventually, this madness will end. But at what cost? Hopefully, President Obama can re-establish the distinction between Iraq and the 9/11 attack. It will take some doing because The Bush Lie has so effectively blurred the line between patriotism and war mongering.

Those of us who understand the meaning of 9/11 will never forget. We will move on, but we will never forget.

DAP: An Internet Discussion Among Black Men

Glenn: What does DAP mean? I know there are two flavors of DAP that I'm familiar with (there might be more)

1. This is what we called a ceremonial greeting with our hands when brothers met or greeted each other. It was very prominent in the military, and on the streets. "Give me some DAP"

2. This what we called certain behaviors by brothers. Like, a certain walk, we say that brother is walking with a DAP, "Look at him Dap" or even the way brothers talk, or look ("Man! that brother got DAP")

It's all good, but exactly what is DAP? Does it stand for something? Do the letters D, A, and P stand for an acronym? What would the modern day equivalent of DAP be? Is DAP still relevant, or has it faded out like the words "Right On!" or "Solid"? This came up while watching "A Murder of Crows"…when Cuba was walking from his jail cell, we noticed "He always walked with a DAP" Help me out with this one. I remember I asked a question about "Playing the Dozen" and

I was given a deep history of it's origin, I didn't realize it was more than just a phrase. Does DAP have a similar history?

David: I searched everywhere and the best I found came from answers.com - at least it made sense to me. *Dap: A complicated and unique hand shake devised by African Americans in Vietnam as a demonstration of racial pride. Quickly picked up by non African Americans and eventually a common form of greeting. It came back to the United States with many of the veterans and became widespread for more than a decade.* ...but I really wouldn't know about that personally --- I was just a toddler when all that was going on.

Joseph: I know back home where I'm from, when the guys say to each other, 'Gimme some daps' it usually means 'slap me five' or the two people hi-five one another in a form of agreeing with one another on a joke or some comment that was made. Now as far as brothers walking with DAP, I call that the soul walk that most brothers have that's typical of African-American males. Some walk with a deeper dip in theirs than others. lol! Do you walk with a DAP Glenn? My barber says we walk like that because of slavery...the anchor ball and chain clamped on one foot made us "drag" that foot thus causing us to walk with a dip in our step.

Kenyada: It's just a word, like thousands of other words blacks have created over centuries. It's OUR word, and one of the things that happens when brothers are grouped together in a foreign land, fighting for something that no one understood. DAP began as slapping five, but it evolved quickly into much, much more. When I left Nam, the DAP was about 8 or 9 steps of handshake. By the time my brother went over there, a few years later, he came back with a 5-minute ritual. Blacks had our own world over there.

We were TIGHT, and we took no shit from anyone. This is from my book, "Essays & Open Wounds While Waiting for The APOLOGY:" "We are together. We call each other blood, short for blood brother. It is a form of respect. There are no black strangers in Vietnam; only bloods we haven't met yet. At 19, I am called 'Youngblood' by most. Embraced by the bloods from The City and Philly, and teased by the bloods from the South and the Mid West, I am now a part of an extended family. During my first few weeks "in country," I am schooled about the do's and don'ts. I am told to write home to girlfriends who used to know me. Not to worry, I am informed that no bloods from New York have ever been killed in 'Nam. It's an easy sale; I need to buy it. Weeks pass, I've settled in, and we move on to the next Youngblood who needs to learn the lessons that will keep him alive another day. Wherever he is from, we tell him that no Blood from there ever "bought it" in 'Nam. We are together like never before in the history of African America. From dark-skinned to light-skinned; country boys and inner-city hard heads ....the black man is united in Vietnam. One fist. The Dap, a fraternal greeting that began as a simple handshake, has evolved into something at which white troops can only marvel. Everybody wants Soul in Nam. Whites want to be black; blacks want to be blacker. There is an insulation in blackness; an attitude of indifference. 'It don't mean nuthin', is more than a phrase, it is a commentary on life itself.

We are the throwaways of society. We are the ones for whom no one had time. We are the ones lacking the sophistication to understand our role, but can generally whip the ass of anyone who can. And, at some point, even *that* becomes a point of pride."

Kenyada: Yes, The DAP was an attitude that was later adapted to black style, in general. I feel good when I hear people talking about it. It brings to mind what we were then and, sadly, what we will never be again... TIGHT!

TJazz: Yeah I remember that word also. As soon as David mentioned Vietnam, I was hoping to get your input. I don't know when your brother went into the service, but when I went in, the DAP was up to 15-20 minutes...I kid you not. The one we (my shipmates and I created) lasted about 3 minutes... you're right, it was special, brothers ONLY and everybody else could only stand by as onlookers and marvel at the creativity and synchronization of brotherhood. I never thought about the word itself, when it was presented to me; it was a beautiful thing and didn't need an explanation.

Every ship, of course, had their own, but there was a universal DAP that every brother knew and used to greet others not in their circle (it was probably the original one you guys gave to the rest of the world). The DAP, thanks to the earlier Vets, found it's way onto our streets and into our communities and helped solidify the collective mindset at that time that Black is Beautiful.

I wished we still had the DAP around, or even just the mindset and brotherhood that it spawned. It was truly a beautiful thing to be a part of or to be about. As you stated, "The DAP, a fraternal greeting ...," that's TIGHT my brother...I'll leave it as that.

Kenyada: I keep hoping that someday, the true story of the Bloods in Nam will be told. There are glimpses of it in a couple of films, most notably, "Hamburger Hill" and "Apocalypse Now." But I want to see an entire film dedicated to what happened over there to us. Just talking about it gets me fired up enough to write a little sumthin' sumthin'. Maybe I need to get it done while I still can. Imagine a film titled "The DAP." That truth needs to come out, to show the young brothers what can happen when we have each other's back, looking out for each other. I remember an older dude (maybe 22) saw me about to take a drag on a passed around "roach". He knocked it out of my hand, and told me that if he ever saw me doing dope, he'd kick my ass and the ass of the Negro who passed it to me. From that day on, nobody offered me anything but a ride in a Jeep. The DAP was about so much more than a greeting, although that's what we all accepted it to be. It was OurStory, y'know? It said something about our history, even the bad stuff. And it said something about our future. For the first time in my life I wasn't afraid of anything - the cops, the teachers, the adults in general... In Vietnam, of all places, I became fearless. And it was because of the nurturing cocoon of The Bloods.

Glenn: Deep statements... I would love to see it, even if it was a documentary...Seeing brothers doing the Dap was awesome, and the thing about that...you could "feel" it even if you weren't the one dapping.

Kenyada: Black men can feel it because it speaks to both our pain and our triumph. DAP also compelled us to feel a "one-ness" with our heritage. Admittedly, a part of the DAP mystique lied in the fact that it befuddled whites so much, making them feel alone by comparison to the brotherhood. But DAP originated as an unspoken "language" of sorts. It was not performed in spite of whites, but rather, without regard for them at all. And it was elevated to ritual-level as it traveled around 'Nam, with guys adding bits of their own flavor to it. You should also understand that DAP was only a part of it. Granted, it was the most out front part of the brotherhood, but the real deal in Nam was about the brotherhood and fraternity we celebrated as being black men. For the first time in our history, there were no divisive elements - no light-skinned/dark-skinned schisms; no middle class/ghetto differences. We were one people.

Can you imagine leaving that kind of nurturing, caring environment, and then landing in the States a few hours later? I felt like the Brother From Another Planet the first time I spoke to a black man in passing, and he looked at me with suspicion and loathing. That harsh awakening was like a splash of ice water in the face.

It's been 40 years, but I've never forgotten what I discovered in 'Nam. I will take those memories to my grave. It's something that no one - black or white - can ever take from me.

Open Letter to George W. Bush, Lame Duck

October 5, 2008

Yo' Bush, you have one month left before the election that will make your presidency an ugly pimple on the butt of American History, but for the young Americans you've killed in Iraq. You will leave office in disgrace on January 20th, but I wonder if your Texas-size ego will allow you that kind of realization. The fact that the John McCain campaign cannot distance itself far enough from you, should tell you something. But that would require a brain. And if you had one, you would have come up with something better than "weapons of mass destruction" as a way to tie Iraq to Afghanistan.

The way in which you quickly morphed the War on Terrorism into the War in Iraq wasn't even clever. Did you think we weren't looking? If you didn't have Daddy issues, you would never have invaded Iraq. In fact, the capture of Saddam Hussein was all about proving your worth to your father, wasn't it? In other words, you've killed those 4,000 young men and women for no reason beyond your own inadequacy as a son. Though you've tried to blur the facts with blind patriotism, we know that if they didn't die in Afghanistan, they died for nothing.

We see evidence that you are now trying to sweep the trash (your legacy) into a neat little pile to sell to McCain voters before November. The problem is that there's only so much bullshit you can stack before it leans, then falls under its own weight. Besides, there's no way to sweep 4,000 American lives under the rug, not that you haven't tried. Some Commander in Chief! That title is a joke when it's associated with your name. The term was carried over from a bygone era when leaders actually were the heroes we followed into battle. They led by example, not from a cushioned perch in somebody's Oval Room. But what did you know about war, Mr. President? You ducked and dodged your way around a commitment to fight in Vietnam, only to have your Daddy buy you a presidency. You make "president" a lower-case word for the first time in the history of this country.

BLACK LOVE

"You introduced yourself, she responded with fresh conversation... She touched your arm to make a point. ...You were free-falling from cloud to cloud, and hoping that she would find a way to touch you again."

Keeping the Love You Make: A Black Man's Guide

When you're looking for love, you think you will recognize it if you see it. And then you fall in love, and have to fumble for the words to describe it. Love shows you - sometimes in glittering detail - everything you didn't know about yourself. At best, love is like magic. The smarter and quicker you are to grasp the concept, the more you are fooled by the trick. You're traveling along in a loving relationship, secure in the knowledge that if it all falls apart tomorrow, you could handle it. And then it falls apart tomorrow - and you realize you can't.

Control is usually the first casualty of love. And if it's really love, you surrender it willingly. You met her when you were least likely to meet someone. Your defenses were inoperable; warning alarms were in standby mode. Your life was a gridlocked matrix of wall-to-wall things to do. The job, the needy friends, the family on the answering machine... there was no room. But there she stood, unhurried and uncluttered, with so much free space surrounding her. You knew that if you didn't speak to her, you would never see her again.

You introduced yourself, and she responded with fresh conversation and exquisite facial reactions. Each of you were interested in listening to what the other had to say. You knew immediately that she was special, and you sensed that the vibe was mutual. With no script and no flight plan, you lost track of time and space. You had heard that it could be like this, but you never believed it. Standing there, seemingly in the center of a merry-go-round, she touched your arm to make a point. Suddenly you were old friends, with a past and a future. Ashford & Simpson songs made sense... "you're all I need to get by..." You were free-falling from cloud to cloud, and hoping that she would find a way to touch you again.

And so it begins. Man meets woman. Man pursues woman... until she catches him. Old joke, sure, but not entirely inaccurate. The basic concept is universal. Men and women are attracted to each other in many ways – physically, intellectually, and spiritually. It's all about chemistry, and the right chemistry can be a very delicate balance – something that wise men will not seek to disturb, despite the temptation.

Keeping the Love You Make

Guys, as we get older, we begin to understand a few things about love (if we are wise and observant). Firstly, it's not just about making love; it's about keeping the love you make. You must first accept certain givens:

The facets of a woman are much like the facets of a diamond, and as different as snowflakes. Our problem is that most of us don't hang in there long enough to witness her in the changing light of our love. When a woman loves you, she may allow herself to fulfill your every need and comply with your every wish. But as tempting as that may sound, we should never allow her to become my-man compliant. As soon as she does, her occupancy in our heart has over stayed its freshness date, and we prepare to move on in search of something less attainable.

The Delicate Balance

When you finally find love, you're compelled to erase all boundaries and come together as "one." One couple. One family. Your friends and family become her friends and family. Well, not if you want to continue to be attracted to each other. Her friends and family - and her relationships with them - have helped to make her the woman that she is, and you don't want to mess with that formula. She should continue her relationships with her friends and, if you're wise, you won't try to ease your way into that unique circle. Today's woman is a product of many influences, and if your goal is to maintain a loving relationship with her, you need to respect certain boundaries – even if she gives you a pass to enter. Insist that she keep in touch with her family and friends. Don't put yourself in the role as a substitute. She will need you to comfort her in times when those very same friends and family frustrate and disappoint her. So stay clear of the outside madness and be her safe haven from it all.

The Marriage License

If you are married, where is your marriage license? If it's in a drawer or filed away in a folder, take it out. Find a beautiful frame and display it proudly in a prominent location where everyone can see it.

You have a license to love each other. Never forget that you are a professional. I was interviewed for a local television show and as she looked around my den preparing camera angles, the show's producer noted that my marriage license was hanging up on the wall like it was a degree or something. I told her that we considered our marriage license to be the equivalent of any historic document. And though we relish our individuality, we are very proud members of a union of love and trust. Display your marriage license so that whenever you happen to look at it, it motivates you to never take your marriage for granted.

Turf Wars and Boundaries

It's important to establish boundaries that protect your relationship from outside interference. There should be a no-fly zone over the sanctity of your relationship – No job, no relatives, no friends, and no adult children. You've got to carve, sometimes chisel, out a place that's just for you and her. It won't be easy because it will seem like everyone wants a piece of you. It's almost as if they have worked out a schedule for your time and they have consulted with everyone else… but you.

Nancy Reagan was onto something with her "just say no" campaign. It may not work in every aspect of your life, but it can be vital in dealing with people who don't respect your boundaries.

"Adult" children – I use quotes because I'm not sure they're really adults – can be the worst perpetrators. They feel that you owe them their lives, and yours, too. Never let them dictate their place in your life. Of course, you must first ensure that you actually have a life. One of the most important boundaries is the bedroom boundary. Here's a list of the activities that should take place in your bed:

- Making Love
- Sleeping

Your bed is not for eating (well, within reason), working, reading, watching TV or talking on the telephone. Your bed is no place for children, or pets, in-laws and conversational friends. Your bed is private property, belonging to you and your woman. This is not negotiable. Make the mistake of moving over for a child who "can't sleep," and you will regret it for the rest of your life together.

Remember, it's not their room, it's yours. I don't care if your Great Dane has the rule of the entire house. His domain ends where yours begins – at the threshold of your bedroom. And don't think that elaborate schemes won't be plotted in order to gain entry to your bedroom. But that's why they make keyed locks. Trust has nothing to do with it. This is your bedroom, and all bets are off when it comes to personal privacy.

Two Individuals vs. The Couple

Everyone knows that approximately 50% of all marriages end in divorce. Many of those marriages suffered the inevitable consequences of falling prey to The Couple syndrome – lost identity. And when the relationship begins to go south, the couple cannot recover the lost ground because they've forgotten the original ingredients of attraction; the original chemistry that brought them together in the first place.

The alternative to becoming a Couple is to remain two individuals in love. That which defines each individual should not change during the entire course of the relationship. As each of you grow within the relationship, boundaries should be maintained. She should maintain her own money, bank accounts, and financial responsibilities. She should have her own telephone number and e-mail account. A woman should keep her mystery. Falling in love is magical, and your woman is a magician, but you should never feel the need to look behind the curtain. A wise man doesn't want to know everything about his woman. Let her maintain those personal characteristics that are uniquely hers. There are two things you never want to see – how the sausage is made, and how your woman does what she does. Just be thankful that you are the recipient of that knowledge.

Those men who are controlling in their relationships rarely enjoy a lasting love with one woman. They initiate a mad dash in the search to "know" everything about their women, but when they accomplish that goal, they quickly lose interest. The irony is that you will never know everything about her, only what she allows you to know. Don't fight it. She will remain more attractive to you as an individual than she will as your better half.

Another Woman

From time to time, you will attract the attention of "Another Woman." You know her. She's the attractive woman shopping at the bookstore, or having lunch at the mall. Your eyes meet, and there is a momentary connection. She smiles and you return her smile, then divert your attention elsewhere. The gesture both acknowledges her and tells her that you're not the one. If she's the woman you think she is, she will continue with her day. If she heads in your direction, she's NOT the woman you first thought she was. And it's not even that she's a threat; she's simply a waste of time.

Too many men fail to understand the dynamic of Another Woman. We think it's all about US when, truthfully, it's all about the man she sees in us – a self-confident man, who carries himself well. Every time Another Woman acknowledges you, she is really acknowledging the work and time that your woman – and/or some other woman – has invested in you. The compliment, then, is not yours - it belongs to someone else. So get over yourself, and politely fend off any potential misunderstanding. The fact that you attracted her should be the pay off. You've still got it! Now wrap it up and take it home.

The Pressure Cooker

A relationship between a man and woman is a potential pressure cooker, and you are allowed to release some steam every now and then. The most successful relationships have a built-in pressure valve – it's called Sleep. Once you sleep on it, you may even forget the most salient points of your argument. Disagreement is healthy for a relationship. Ideally you may dream of having a Stepford Wife - one who says and does everything your heart desires. But it can be very tiring to have to think for two. Besides, a man needs the challenge of having a woman with her own mind. Sure, she will say and do things occasionally that simply drive you up a wall, but the alternative is complete and utter boredom, with a predictable robot that waits for your next command.

Sometimes in the midst of a disagreement, you will suddenly realize that you are – dare I say it - wrong. It is for those times that you will need to develop an exit strategy that will allow you to withdraw without necessarily admitting defeat [Like Nixon tried to do in Vietnam].

They say that sharks "smell" blood in the water. A woman can sense the exact moment when her man knows he's fighting a losing battle. Stepping down from your argument, then, is best accomplished gradually. Slowly, but surely, adopt one single point that your woman makes, without her seeing the move. Magicians call it "slight of hand." Husbands call it "the oakey-doke,"

OK, I've avoided it as long as I could. I know, I know; it's difficult territory for even the bravest of men, but if you really want to find true happiness, you cannot avoid The C-Word.

Commitment

There are those who believe that Love will take care of itself, with very little investment from us. That may work for awhile… like the first few minutes. But most lovers soon find out that no investment results in no return, and very little investment produces very little return.

Commitment is similar to sexual surrender, where you just let go of yourself and trust your partner to be there for you if you fall or fail. The struggle is in reaching that point of trust, and risking all despite the fear. Men get scared, too, and it's all right to be afraid; just not to the point where it constricts your movement forward.

Each of us tends to want a guarantee before we commit, and nothing short of a guarantee will allow us to make that move. There are several possible reasons for that fear. We won't commit to one woman, because there's always a chance that the next one we meet will be… prettier, or smarter, or sexier (fill in the blank). And we're so busy looking over our shoulders for her, that we miss the opportunity to really appreciate the woman we have right in front of us.

Then there are those of us who are never quite certain whether a woman loves us or our money, car, house, clothes… (Fill in that blank, too). I suspect that early in the relationship those guys went out of their way to impress the woman with those things, using them to separate themselves from her other suitors. And then when she starts to demonstrate her affection, the guy is never quite sure of her motivation. The solution is simple – bait your hook with your personal attributes, instead of your gear. In order to accomplish that goal, you must first be comfortable within yourself, without flaunting your trinkets. Separate yourself from your stuff. If you wish to find something real, you'll need to be real.

Besides, today's black woman is very likely to have her own money, car, house, clothes, etc. She is quite self-sufficient and does not need a man's identity from which to carve out her own. So be prepared to meet her on level ground as an equal, or keep on steppin'.

But, again, how can you be sure? My Brother, if you are looking for guarantees, try Sears, not Sienna. She may love you 20 years from today, but she may also break your heart tomorrow. It's the chance you take; it's the chance we all take. Man up! You could build a wall or a moat around yourself, which would keep you from being hurt. But it would also keep you from being touched.

Guys, we waste a lot of time and effort stumbling and staggering from lustful conquest to lustful conquest. But what have we won? When you truly love a woman, you don't want to conquer her; you want to conquer together with her. Then you both win.

A good woman is a beautiful flower that opens up to you one petal at a time. She requires what I call RAPTURE – Respect, Attention, Patience, Technique, Understanding, Reassurance and Endurance. First of all, if any of those requirements need an explanation, you don't belong at the grown-up's table. And if you are not ready to meet those requirements, please don't waste her time. If you are ready, be ready also to make that commitment to her alone, because you cannot possibly meet these requirements for one woman and have enough left over to fulfill the same needs of another – not if you're doing it correctly.

Romance should never be confused with "gettin' some." Often romance is the investment you make that will translate into that kind of dividend later. Romance is an on-going state of being; a 24/7 place of comfort and forgiveness. Guys whose women consider them romantic are generally considerate, thoughtful, flattering and sharing. Men don't necessarily need to plan the romance. The most genuine romance is an environment you establish rather than a deed you orchestrate.

A romantic man is a good listener who is not waiting for a moment to hijack the conversation and re-direct it to him. Listening is more than hearing, when it comes to a woman. Feeling for, and caring about, what you hear is also important. How many times have you held a conversation with a woman and not really listened to her, catching only partial points of interest? If she is worth talking with, she is worth your undivided attention.

There are all kinds of intimacy that we as men miss out on, due to our inability to listen. A woman will open up to you if she feels that you are really listening to her, and from that affirmation, a deeper trust will develop, leading to intimacy miles away from the nearest bed.

Keeping the Love you make is the goal. Many of us enter into a relationship with an exit strategy already mapped out before we sit down.

TV talk show host Ellen DeGeneres once asked guest Will Smith what was the secret that he and wife, Jada Pinkett Smith, had for a successful 10-year marriage. Mr. Smith, usually always ready with a quip or punchline, remarked quite seriously, "What I found is divorce just can't be an option," It's really that simple… So a huge part of the success for [Jada] and I is that we just removed the other options." I could not agree more with that assessment. You have to say at some point, whatever it takes, we are going to be together. If something needs fixing, we have to fix it together. And it's not easy to make that kind of commitment when other options are available, which is what Will Smith noted. "We're like, 'We're going to be together one way or the other so we might as well try to be happy.' " In this day and era, those words are profound.

Ajax Park

We called it Ajax Park, but we never knew why. Legend has it that the crane used in the park's construction had the name Ajax on its side. And then there's the story that before construction, there was a billboard in the vacant lot that advertised Ajax Cleanser. Of course, the park's real name is Charles Drew Memorial Park, dedicated in memory of Dr. Charles R. Drew, an African American. The storage of blood in plasma form has saved untold lives since Drew brought the process forward in the 1930's, and he created the model for blood and plasma storage that is still used by the Red Cross today.

Located in the South Ozone Park community of Jamaica, Queens, Ajax was more of a playground than a park. It contained three full basketball courts, six handball courts and two major leagued-sized baseball diamonds. In fact, in the 1950's, a soon-to-be National League team (the Metropolitans, or Mets) held some of their tryout games at Ajax, where semi-pros played every weekend.

In 1955, my family moved to Queens from the Bedford-Stuyvescent section of Brooklyn, a neighborhood of attached brownstone homes, but no play areas in sight. Our new home was located in an established middle class, tree-lined neighborhood, directly across the street from Ajax Park. It wasn't just a different neighborhood; it was a different world.

I spent most of my adolescence on the basketball courts of Ajax. Summer, winter, fall and spring, but especially in the summer. Summers at Ajax were always special. There'd be bid whist on the picnic table, checkers, Nok-Hockey tournaments… We'd play handball, too, and the girls of Ajax could play with the best in the City. But mostly it was about basketball. In the early 1960's, Ajax basketball was an addiction. Everyone who lived within a few miles was drawn to the park. There would be bicycles parked along the fences of the courts. No locks, no chains - there were no thieves among us.

There was no gang violence because, quite simply, there were no gangs. There was, however, a sense of belonging - we belonged to Ajax Park. There was, in essence, a family structure; a sense of order. We had every age group represented - the over 20's, under 20's teens. There were no little kids, primarily because there was nothing for a little kid to do at Ajax. No swings, slides, monkey bars or sand boxes. Those features were down the street at Ajax's sister playground, Comet, a named gleened from Ajax, another cleanser.

The "Parkies," or park attendants, of Ajax kept the playground clean, landscaped and safe. I remember a Parkie named Mr. Guess, who took such pride in his work. One of his main tasks was removing the weeds from between the cobblestones that ran along the inside of the sidewalk. It was a 10-foot width of cobblestones that encircled the entire playground, easily a half-mile. He was meticulous in his approch to his work, and I watched him, and spoke with him sometimes as he worked. He lived in the neighborhood and, therefore, served as another positive black male role model in a community that had more than its share.

Much of the sense of order at Ajax can be attributed to our parents and our teachers at surrounding schools like Shimer Junior High School, and Public School 123. Down the street and around the corner from Ajax, Shimer Junior High School, was the middle school inherited by most everyone in the neighborhood after graduating the nearby elementary school, P.S. 123.

Besides its reputation for being a place where recent elementary school grads could look forward to getting their asses kicked, Shimer was the closest thing we knew to being a grown-up. We would enter into our teen years at some point along the halls of Shimer, and the next step would be high school. It was the first time that we would receive a schedule of classes that we would have to follow on our own, and arrive to each class on time. For many of us, it was our first glimpse of personal responsibility, wherein there was no adult looking over our shoulder to make sure we did the right thing. We knew that if we screwed up, we would not suffer the consequences as a class. Our screw ups, and the punishment meted out for them, were individual and personal.

The teachers at Shimer didn't take any crap from anyone. Even the tough guys behaved themselves under the watchful eyes of the teachers. And for the first time in our academic environment, we saw black teachers in greater numbers than ever before. It was almost as if Shimer was the place they were all sent to keep us in line. Of course, the previous year's experience of having Mrs. Harper as my 6th Grade teacher, had prepared me well for black teachers.

Mrs. Lorraine Harper, was Negro while everyone else was still "Colored," and I'll bet she went Black before any of the rest of us felt comfortable with that term. Of course, my problem was that we shared the same last name, and my classmates never tired of reminding me of it. Our class was 6-1, the top class at our grade level, and Mrs. Harper never let us forget it. We only had three white kids in our class – Thomas Glembocki, George Gardener and Theodore White. Whenever the class misbehaved, Mrs. Harper would keep us seated after the 3 o'clock bell. But she would first allow Thomas, George and Teddy to go home. We all knew what we were in for, and resigned ourselves to The Black Lecture.

Mrs. Harper would reiterate the importance of education, particularly to blacks in this country. She told us that we had to be smarter and better equipped than whites in order to be considered equal. We had never heard that equation from any other teacher, but we accepted it.

The incident that brought it all together for me was the day we had a fire drill at 2:45 pm, just before the end of the day. Mrs. Harper had entrusted me with a folder of paperwork that she asked me to carry with me, so that she could leave without returning to the class after the fire drill. When the fire drill bell rang, I left with the class, forgetting the folder, and I walked home after the drill. Once home I changed my clothes and was ready to go to Ajax to play basketball. As I was leaving my yard, Mrs. Harper pulled up in her car. She asked about her folder, and I told her that I forgot it in the classroom. She told me - with a look I dared not question - to get into her car.

Mrs. Harper didn't speak as she drove back to the school. We got out of her car and she walked me upstairs to the classroom. She opened the door and I retrieved the folder. She didn't say a word as we headed back to her car. As I stood there on the sidewalk watching her get into her car, she told me, "As you walk back home, you will have time to think about personal responsibility. When someone gives you a task, it is your responsibility to complete it." Something clicked in my brain when I heard her say "task." Up until that moment, all I remembered having were "chores" – the kind of stuff your parents give you to do. But "Task" sounded more adult; more grown-up. As I walked home, I thought about what Mrs. Harper had said. I think it meant more to me because it wasn't said in a classroom. It was said on the street; in the real world. I half-ran, half-walked back to the neighborhood, and quickly slipped across the street to Ajax. I did not want my parents to know that I was on Mrs. Harper's shit list – at least not that day.

My teacher probably had no idea how much of a defining moment it was for me. I didn't realize it myself until many years later when

I heard myself repeating her words to my own son. I just smiled to myself as I thought back to that day, the first time I can remember understanding the concept of personal responsibility. Mrs. Harper stayed on at P.S. 123 where she continued to teach the teachers in her new role as principal.

Mrs. Harper prepared me for what I was to find at Shimer - more no-nonsense black teachers than I had ever seen before. And there was one, who stood out above all the rest - Mr. Nathan Bright. He was my first black male teacher, and though he was only on my schedule for Gym, his impact on me and the other young black men in his classes cannot be overstated. Mr. Bright was the Physical Education teacher, who stressed education as much, if not more, than he taught physical training. Even a seemingly simple game like basketball required one to think, he would tell us. "Why is a jump shot an effective offensive weapon?" he would ask. While several white broadcasters were always making note of the natural ability of black players, Mr. Bright compelled us to study the game and use our heads when we play. He helped us to understand that the best players don't just "play" the game, they "think" it, as well. There is no student of Mr. Bright who did not benefit from his wisdom, and there was never any doubt about the path to be taken once we listened to this man. We took his life lessons along with us, both on and off the courts of Ajax where, along with the support of our parents, we remained focused on the future.

On November 7, 1960 the United Federation of Teachers went on strike. For the first time we saw teachers walking in picket lines and carrying signs in front of Shimer and other schools. I'll never forget it because the always dapper Mr. Bright, in his suit and tie, looked much more dignified and astute than anyone I'd ever seen in a picket line.

Like many of my friends, I thought that the strike was going to be a day, or a week, off from school, but my parents made me go to school anyway. Shimer was only a few blocks away, and when I got there, I saw all of the teachers, including black teachers – Mr. Bright, Mr. Periman, Mr. Clairborne, Mr. Bantam, Mrs. Burnett and others - with their signs. There were also reporters and TV cameras, and it was so cool that it was a media event. Like an idiot, I mistook it as a chance to hang out with the teachers, because it was almost as if they were protesting school itself – and I could really relate to that on some juvenile level. I approached Mr. Bright smiling, and walked along side him… for about one step. And then he looked at me in all seriousness and told me to get my butt into school. Dejected, I walked to the entrance, and Mr. Bright called out to me: "Harper, your education never takes a day off!"

It's strange how moments like those never leave you. I saw Mr. Bright again 46 years later, at the annual Ajax Park/Shimer JHS Reunion in 2006. I recalled that story, and I could tell that he didn't remember our exchange, but he was happy that it meant so much to me that I remembered.

Many of us were fortunate to have had so many influential and positive black male role models right there in the neighborhood to supplement the teachings of our fathers, grandfathers and uncles. And some of us would graduate and move on to John Adams High School in Ozone Park, where there were no black teachers or guidance counselors at all. So our experiences and exposure to the teachers at P.S. 123 and Shimer would have to carry us. Fortunately, those strong black teachers left an indelible impression on me that would serve me well throughout my years at Adams with its all-white teaching staff. I realized that those teachers - regardless of their color - held my education in their hands, and it was my responsibility to take it, because no teacher, white or black, was going to give it to me.

Always in the background, Ajax Park offered a secondary family structure for many of us. The different age groups represented older brothers, cousins and uncles - people we looked up to and, in many cases, emulated. The kids in my age group, 12-14, saw black men play together as teams, as well as adversaries, on the basketball courts. We saw black men interact peacefully, and subordinate themselves for the sake of team victory. We witnessed black men winning and losing, and trying again. Those basketball courts were a training ground for so many scenarios that we would later face in life as men.

The first court was hallowed ground. The kids in my age group could play there as long as the older guys weren't around. But as soon as they showed up, it was understood that we would have to move down to another, less important court, even though all three full courts were exactly the same, technically. As my age group grew older, we moved up in the chain of command, and the older guys became the elders of Ajax. Other younger kids replaced us at the lower rung of the Ajax hierarchy, and we treated them with the same amount of respect with which we had been treated - exactly no respect at all.

I remember that feeling well - the first time that I bridged the divide between kid and man. I was shooting around on the second court with a few friends. The players on the first court were short a man.

"Harper! Hey, Harper, you wanna play?" I remember nodding in agreement. I was too nervous to speak. They were asking me to play basketball with them. Me?! With my heart pounding, I trotted over to the first court with a muted smile. On my way, I briefly glanced over my shoulder to my friends, who remained on the second court. They had that look on their faces that told me I had crossed over in their minds. I didn't think that they would ever see me the same way again, until they made the journey for themselves... and eventually they all would. When one played on the first court at Ajax, there was an unspoken sense of ownership in the park itself. People knew your name... and your game. It was a community of play, but it was also a gathering of brothers that gave us each a separate identity as part of a whole - Ajax Park.

At Ajax we learned to appreciate the silence of a clean shot through the hoop. There were no nets on the baskets, so there was no "swish," nothing-but-net sound when the ball went directly into the hoop without touching the rim. And then there was The Pole from which the backboard was mounted. The eight-inch diameter hardened steel was buried deep in asphalt, rock and earth, and it wasn't moving. It was not offset; it was right there on the court, and presented quite a problem for visitors who were unaware of its presence. The Pole could also serve as a 4th man, screening defenders away. We found that we could float across the baseline, from one side of the basket to the other. Either the defender stopped pursuing us, or we heard the unmistakable "clunk" of bone meeting steel.

Year 'round full–court and half-court games were played dating all the way back to the 1950's, but it was the mid-1960's through '70's that were the essence of Ajax Park. I missed some of it during my military enlistment and tours of duty in Vietnam, but when I returned in 1968, it was almost as if I had never left. The Ajax of my dreams, that had kept me sane in a combat zone, was still alive and thriving.

The players were characters, really, known throughout the neighborhood. Two of those characters were the Tribble Twins – Martin and Melvin – and they were predators on the court. Both had great jump shots and each could keep a defender running all day long. A visitor from another city once asked me, "How do you tell them apart?" I chuckled, "It's in the jump shot. When Melvin makes his long jumper right over your defense, he will laugh right in your face. Martin is kinder… he will turn around, and laugh at you, quietly so as not to offend you."

The world of art had its Picasso; Ajax had Tito, and his game was pure artistry. It is said that some basketball players have a 360-degree view of the court, during a game. Tito had all of that… plus an aerial view. Farnell, on the other hand, played a power game – great leaping ability and the strength to pull down seemingly unreachable rebounds. If he went after a rebound, and your arm happened to be between the ball and his hand… "Oops, sorry 'bout that, but I hear they're doing amazing things these days with prosthetics." My game was mostly finesse. I took the path of least likely resistance. I had some "hops," combined with a fall-away jump shot that, when hot, could not be stopped by straight up defense.

Combined, Tito, Farnell and I, had played hundreds – perhaps thousands - of 3-man games at Ajax, but until that fateful day in 1971, we had never played on the same 3-man team. Farnell had the first choice, and he chose Tito, of course. The other captain selected a player, and then Farnell chose me, next-door neighbor of 16 years. So that was the team and, as it turned out, each of us on that team brought his A-game to the park that day. No other team – consisting of some of the very best regulars at Ajax - could beat us. Those games were sheer poetry for the way in which each of our games blended with and complimented that of the other. I once went up real high for a rebound, and found Farnell already there… and smiling. Tito was a magician with the basketball. A defender could not guard him too closely for fear that Tito would drive around him, split the defense and dish it off to me or Farnell. We won every game we played that day, totaling 10 or 11, and we were very tired. So it was agreed that we would play one last game. And it was probably because it was the last game that each of us rose to the occasion, pouring it on to give everyone something to think about. When it was over, Tito, Farnell and I threw the ball to the next team, walked off the court, and never looked back. It wasn't planned; it just happened that way – like the last walk-off scene on "The Mod Squad."

My most memorable moment at Ajax was on Friday, November 22, 1963. John Adams High School had mid-term exams, and a few of us – Joe Scott, Roger Smith, Bill Gordon and I - who had already taken our tests earlier in the week, decided to go to Ajax to play some ball. That morning, the Parkie had raised the flag up the flag pole, as he did every morning. But a few hours later, it was strange to see him lowering the flag. So after a game, we walked over to him and asked about the lowering of the flag to half-mast. He clearly had tears in his eyes when he told us that President Kennedy had just been shot and the President was dead. We all ran home, confused and afraid. For the rest of the weekend, Ajax was like a ghost town, as we all stayed home glued to our black and white TV sets. JFK's assassination was my generation's "9/11," and our lives - as well as our country - would change forever.

A little over three years after that day at Ajax, I found myself in the middle of Vietnam. Growing up in the supportive atmosphere at Ajax Park had prepared me well for what I found in The Nam. I have never been surrounded by so many black men, from all over the country, who felt so much a part of each other. Like the players of Ajax, The Bloods in 'Nam offered an almost family-like structure of comfort and caring for one another. There were the elders, who were 20-22. They had been there the longest and knew how to stay alive. They passed that information freely to the new men as soon as we departed the airplane.

Over 400 years of opression had made black men suspicious of everyone, particularly each other. But Vietnam changed all that. We were in a war zone, and danger lurked around almost every corner. But even black strangers were treated like brothers in The 'Nam. I've written about this often, particularly in my first book, because it was the most profound experience of my life. To my knowledge, African American men had never been as together as we were in 'Nam. We certainly have never been as together since. And had it not been for the formative years I spent at Ajax, I'm not sure that I could have appreciated the relationships of the The Bloods in Vietnam. That's why I attribute any success I've enjoyed to the mindset I acquired early in life - you win, or you lose and try again, but you never give up.

Every year since 1990, the Ajax Park family reunites at the park. We've all grown older, and put on a few pounds, but that competitive fire still lives on in each of us, just beneath the surface. And when we greet each other - coming from all over the country - we can't help but make note of those who have passed on, which is appropriate because that's how the reunions began 18 years ago.

Wayne Butler who, like myself, grew up living across the street from Ajax Park, had died in an automobile accident. Friends Val Farnell and Ty Mormon decided to host a memorial to Wayne. It was well attended by everyone from the old neighborhood, and it has grown every year since then. Each year we may lose a few, and gain a few, but the love still grows. There are some who mean so much to us that it would seem impossible to continue without them, but we do – we must, because we know they would have wanted us to continue.

When we make that pilgrimage to Ajax Park every year, it's about more than the memories. It's a recharging of the old batteries; a clearing of the cobwebs. The first time I returned was in 2006, 29 years after I left New York. Ajax had changed – an additional basketball court, new bench seating near the courts. The entrance to the park had been widened and wheel chair access had been added to the rest rooms.

The baseball diamonds – once manicured to a fault – were overrun and the turf in the outfield had been torn and dug up by new immigrants who felt they had an unalienable right to play their native games, no matter how much of Ajax they destroyed in the process. These Cricket Nazis apparently travel from baseball field to baseball field ripping out pieces of their newly adopted country. They could not have gotten away with that back in the day, not under the watchful eyes of our welcoming committee consisting of Big Freddie, Robin LaBorde and Big Pope. Naw, they would have run back to Pakistan in a hurry.

When we lost Wayne Butler so early in his life, I think it made us all pause for a moment of reflection, no matter where we were around the country. It was a wake up call for the rest of us. We grew up in a generation that felt indestructible and invincible. And then suddenly we were not. Wayne's death hit home because he was one of us, so it was personal.

They say that when a friend or family member dies, at some point you forget his face, and must rummage through old photographs in order to recall his image in memories. Not so with Wayne Butler, or any of the other Ajax family members we have lost. Their faces, voices and personalities remain as crisp and unforgettable in death as they were in life. And maybe that's because they were larger than life when they lived. Wayne, Robbie Peterson, Doug Perry, Leslie "Legs" Wright, Cheryl Beauford, Pope and the others – they are all still with us, every step of the way. And we are the better for it.

I don't know how many more Ajax/Shimer Reunions I will see. Tomorrow is not promised. But I do know that when I die, my friends won't have to travel to a faraway gravesite to "visit" me. My ashes will be right there in between and beneath the cobblestones at the fence, near the first court at Ajax... and I'll have "next."

Love, Real and Remembered

Once upon a time, there were beautiful, fully orchestrated love songs. The first R&B recording to use violins was The Drifter's "There Goes My Baby" in 1958. Twenty years later, when synthesizers began replacing strings in the studio, it may well have started us on a path of substituting what is Real for what is synthetic - in our music and, perhaps, in our lives as well.

As keyboard synthesizers were substituted for woodwind instruments, orchestras evolved into two-man bands. Real drummers need not apply, as long as someone in the house could program a computer. (Somehow, James Brown shouting, "give the Programmer some" wouldn't quite do it for me). Maybe my era has moved on. When Eddie Kendricks died in what seemed like minutes from David Ruffin, and they, in turn, called for Melvin Franklin an "hour" later. I started packing for my journey. Surely they would not leave me here alone to fend off R Kelly and the gangstas; condemned to the medieval torture of remakes and keyboard samples.

Where reality is Truth, we have slowly switched over to truth-with-an-asterisk. Co-opted. Watered down ...like a Nielsen survey determined that we could deal with a whole lot less artistic and emotional substance in our daily diet. And children ask each other,

"Are you for real?" while soda manufacturers substitute a euphemism called high fructose corn syrup for real sugar ...and have the nerve to hawk it as The Real Thing. In the age of wonder bras and collagen lips, they've added "hips" to panties, prosthetic organs to men's briefs ...worn by those who cruise nightclubs, looking for something Real. But then, they paint the grass green in some sports stadiums and we call it The Beauty of Mother Nature. I'm beginning to believe that, in some weird way, it's all connected ...like Diana Ross could tighten her weave, and the blue grass would swell on the foothills of Kentucky. Even our personal relationships are now suspect. Many men and women lease each other for a few months at a time, with less documentation than would be required to lease a Hyundai. Few expectations and no real love. But I still dream revolutionary dreams, and share the left side of a king-sized bed with the woman I love (never apart when we have a choice). And we still try to find new ways to say old things ...like, "I Love You."

Some say it is difficult to find someone to love, due to demographic shortages. Perhaps the real deficit is a perceived shortage of Time. Clicking biological clocks abound. Signs of the season's first "crow's feet" are met with double orders of alpha hydroxy lotion. As Baby Boomers turn 50, the younger generations are pulled closer to their own inevitability. And so we are all pushed up against the wall by the crowd watching the parade pass by. The best we can hope for is a way out of this un-Real cul-de-sac daydream; this place of huge, high hedges that we call Love in the 21st Century. That way out must ultimately lead us towards each other.

So I wake up every morning beside the same woman. Each day we set out to prioritize the Search for each other. When everything is working - the Doppler radar, the all-points bulletins, the Armani-sniffing dogs - we connect. And appreciating the enormity of the accomplishment, we fall in love over and over again ...on the same dime.

The menu of Life serves up exquisite pictures of fine wine and delicate cuisine, but most of us settle for a burger and fries ...greasy fries. Been there; done that. And for all the joyful, running-through-the-meadows years of bachelorhood I celebrated - first, as a single man, then later as a divorced, single Dad - I never found the freedom I sought until I ran into the arms of a good woman. Proving once again that, as witty and wise as we think we are, Real Love is smart enough to figure this thing out long before we do, and is probably waiting for us... just around the bend.

Black Love: Choosing the Black Doll

We had it once, like no other group of people on the face of this earth. Despite overt racism that seemed to permeate each and every aspect of our daily lives. Despite the poverty and powerlessness layered upon each other through successive generations, there was always a certain wealth of love that helped us get by. And Lawd, we were a proud people. It was in our style; in our fashion sense, the way we walked down the street. It was in the children of our youth, as they played street games, always striving to win. But it was also in the straightness of their backs as they sat in class, and the swiftness with which they raised their hands with the correct answers.

Love was in our starched white shirts and pressed pleated skirts that Mom laid out for us each school morning. Love accompanied us to school, and it was everywhere else. Love was in our music, too. The silky smooth lyrics of Smokey Robinson, who the Beatles called the world's greatest living poet. Smokey sang about "More Love" so strong it made you want to give it up against the wall under blue lights in the basement.

Yes, we had it all once. The love, the self-respect - pride in ourselves and our people. Where did our love go?

The Supremes' plaintively musical question seems to peek at us from around each corner now. Our personal relationships have become tentative, as we walk into each one like a gunslinger walking into a saloon; looking for a back door through which to escape if the lead starts flying. Love rolls off our tongues so quickly over dinner, yet so swiftly silences itself over the next morning's coffee. Love isn't savored as much as it is touched upon, like a worn turnstile in an old Brooklyn subway station. Turning one click at a time; taking tokens that some people have the nerve to call commitment. Going around in circles, invariably returning to where it all began. That's not the kind of Love we knew - a love that stood for something.

The Love we remember was a journey forward. It had character and purpose. It was stalwart and deeply rooted in morality. Our Love was pristine and lust-driven; part fantasy, but wholly Real. While some of us have never lost sight of such Love, too many of us see it as storybook narrative.

If our interpersonal connections are strained, our network -the love we feel for each other as a people - is in shambles. Where did that love go? We had that once, also. Before we caught that all-expenses-paid excursion cruise to America. Ever since we hit these shores, we have allowed suspicion and distrust to put us at odds with each other. They separated us on the plantation - field Negroes and house Negroes. Though we can blame the Massa for choosing the sides, we must share that blame for letting his impositions enter our psyche.

After slavery, we further separated ourselves along lines of color - light-skinned versus dark-skinned. Of all the ridiculous, self-defeating crap we have ever perpetrated on ourselves, this is a classic. Along comes integration and we further separate ourselves into the haves and the have-nots. There are several variations of that theme still going down today. What were the "You-might-be-ghetto-if" jokes, if not more of the same us-against-them counter-productivity? I missed the point. Perhaps I'm too old; heard too many Rastus-this and Sambo-that jokes in my lifetime. Maybe I'm not sophisticated enough to appreciate the culinary artistry required to slice 'n dice our own people for sport. Forgive me. I was ashamed of those ghetto-putdowns because some of our best and brightest were wasting their time, and our people's trust, in the trivial pursuit of bashing that which is our own - our people. We were the head of the dragon that turns around in mock disdain of its tail - though we are both headed in the same direction together ....or we will stumble and perish together.

We are the descendants of kings and queens. The cradle of humanity rests in the arms of our Motherland. Some of us may buy into that Adam and Eve fabrication - two blond, blue-eyed apple-guzzling, serpent-challenged white folks running around in fig leaves. But I've yet to read about two whites reproducing melanin, the dark pigmentation that gives black, brown, red and yellow folks (and Tiger Woods) their color. I have, however, heard of blacks reproducing blond-haired, blue-eyed albinos whose skin and eyes are extremely sensitive to light. Didn't the Vikings live in dark caves?

HELLO!?

My point is that this is our show. We were stronger than slavery. We are stronger than racism. They have tried to lull us to sleep with crack. Dull our senses with alcohol; wreak havoc on our nervous systems with cocaine derivatives. But our resilience is legend. The common thread woven through 400 hundred years of struggle on this continent has been our Love. These backs will bend, but they will not break. Love stands strong. Our tears, sweat and blood have saturated the earth, yet they will not take root to harvest terminal misery. Love stands invincible.

Don't let anyone tell you that we are not stronger than any obstacle they place before us. We can fight this fight and win, and we don't have to march to Washington. We don't have to take one step. But we must stand. Our men and women must stand together, and administer to our children. And they, in turn must stand up to take the torch. And when that happens, you will see the ground swell, and feel vibrations of volcanic proportions. Fearful, some will flee; charter one-way excursions to Mars. But those of us who hold fast will know the ultimate power of Love reiterated, strength regained.

poem for a lady loved

> i lie here watching you sleep
> so peacefully.   brush your cheek,
> feeling you stir only long enough
> to draw closer   quiet/calm   still.
> still surrendering to your lover
> the last silences
> of well spent passion.
> i know that tomorrow you must return,
> return to black-woman-as-super-heroine.
> i trust that you will sense the malady,
> then soar to save those lesser
> among us, putting the check in the mail
> for life as we know it, while brushing aside

nominations by nobel and pulitzer.
i know you'll pay your respects
to the pope   and pose in the oval room
before noon   at disney world.
you'll make suggestions to the mayo clinic,
and sketch out a plan to save the ozone layer,
while on an herbal tea break from shuttle crew
maneuvers.
but tonight…
            i've got your back,
and the world will have to
take a number
as you slumber
with your cheek against my chest.

IN APPRECIATION

"It was at the completion of the very first senior computer workshop that a dear woman approached me to shake hands. In her hand was a tiny folded piece of paper. As she left left the library, I unfolded the piece of paper, which kept getting larger and larger. It turned out that she had given me a five dollar bill. I will never forget that moment of appreciation."

Website: If You Build It, They Will Come
Mr. Kenyada's Neighborhood (1998-2008)

As MKN takes its place in community history, I want to thank all those who helped me to DO SOMETHING. It's one thing to boldly stand up and step forward, but unless someone stands up with you, your effectiveness will be limited. The list is extensive because it includes those who donated both volunteer time and money to keep the PCs to the People program going and growing.

My wife, Patricia Kenyada, without whose support, encouragement, patience, commitment and dedication to my vision, MKN would not have been possible. My trusted friend of over 30 years, Clara Delay, an MKN stalwart who, despite a hectic schedule, found time to edit both of my books. Glenn Hearn - we were the Batman & Robin of computer literacy in Atlanta... and sometimes, he'd let me play Batman. Dr. Joseph Sessums, Ph.D., a computer science professor at a metro Atlanta college, who volunteered his expertise for our seniors computer workshop. In Lawrence, Kansas, Cynthia Colbert contributed her considerable talents to make MKN the website, a much more stylish place. Roger Ford, aka Six M Connection, connected with us from Memphis, and no one was more dedicated to MKN than Six M, until his untimely death. Robert Harris, J.L. Smith, Renee King, Val Fitchett, Clarence Barnes, Simon Manning-Moon, David Jeffries & America's Mart, William Strong, Sistory & DryerBuzz, Calvin O'Rear, Paul Edwards, Mark Burks, Prince (yes, that Prince) & Love4One Another, Sam's Club at Stonecrest, Kyra James, O. Curtis White, Vickie White, Charisse Boone, Lita McCormick, Connie Sutani, Rhonda Burns, Tamara Harris, Barbara Houston, Hettie Summerlin, Michael Larry, Mr. & Mrs. Feimster, Rose Boggus, Ken Pressley, Kim Lynch, Michael Foster, Mr. & Mrs. Ron Rowe, Cheryl Barker, Lynne Connolly, Darro Wiley and the DeKalb County Public Library, Heath & Lineback Engineers, Inc., Jane Fonda (Yes, that Jane Fonda), Kim Martin, Tuere Bowles, LaShelle White, Ashton Savoy, Ronald Tyson, Symantec, James Smith, Athena Jones, Hattie Kenyada, Darni Bolden, Eunice Kirby, Portia Bolden, Vera Robinson, Anthony Parrish, Anna Leatherwood, Mr. & Mrs. J.L. Smith, United Way, Renee Booker, Mr. & Mrs. Wendell Johnson, Kroger Food Stores, Circuit City, Lisa Crockett,

Phyllis Brower, O'Neil Moss, Elke Davison, Price WaterhouseCoopers, Smith, Gambrell and Russell, Superstation WTBS, Tom Harris Salon, Mr. & Mrs. Aaron Ribner, Self, Glaser & Davis, David Brown, Jay Rice, Mary Gay, Tonya, Yvette Harper, Monique, Ms. Mini, HellyHell, Keva, Queen Bee, Gail Darlington, Mich-Choc, Heritage Printing & Frames, and Myster-E....and now a few community comments selected from the hundreds we received over the years...

Hurray for Mister Kenyada and all those who support him and his philosophy. His insight and dedication to the African-American community is greatly appreciated, I only wish we had more like him to make a difference. My daughter was one of the recipients of his "computers to the people" and it has made a significant impact in her life and her families'. It has opened up a whole world for all of us. The only problem now is everyone in the house wants to use it at the same time, even her father who is totally computer illiterate, now uses it to tap into the web. WE LOVE IT AND YOU, MR. KENYADA!!!!
Michelle Sherard – Lithonia , GA

If YOU ONLY KNEW how this has fueled me on to get my Degree in Microcomputer Specialist. I started late in life to complete my education at age 46 and being an African American Male has been rough over the years, but I WILL make it. Thanks to you, Brother!!!!!!
Melvin E. Carmichael - Decatur , GA

I'd just like to offer my encouragement and gratitude to you for not only recognizing the importance of an informed society, but doing something about it. Yours in Brotherhood
Wilton George - Syracuse , New York

Mr. Kenyada, your website is the most inspiring I have ever viewed on my screen. Keep up the good work and may the Lord bless you. I have told so many of my friends about your website.
Lynn Johnson - Penllyn , PA

Read about your site in the AJC article. Took a quick gander at it and want to add my compliments on such a POSITIVE effort. I wish you

MUCH continued success. Dr. Joseph L. Sessum, Ph.D. [professor of Computer Science] Kennesaw, GA

I think this is FANTASTIC!!!! It's high time that someone took the time to show an interest in the welfare of the black community. Keep up the good work. Vanessa Bonner - Atlanta , GA

Mr. Kenyada, I read your article in the AJC. The information in the article confirmed some of my thoughts of the computer literacy level of our folk. From my first hand survey your reports are pretty accurate. I usually ask my clients are they on the net. You know the answer. Your article is timely because I am sure it is going to wake up a few folks. Sometimes it takes pioneers such as yourself to bring us into reality. Keep up the good work! Ralph E. Williams - College Park , GA

Mr. Kenyada, I heard about you through a recent article in the Atlanta Journal/Constitution, which provided information on a recent study showing the disparity in computer and Internet access among African Americans. I'm glad to know your site exists. I will want to get in touch with you regarding a proposal to establish a community technology center in Atlanta Empowerment Zone.
Al Lane - Atlanta , GA

Hi! I found your WEB SITE address on the Asahi Evening this morning. I have been interested in African-Americans. Mr. Richard Kenyada, I want to know more about African- Americans in the United States .
Hiroshi Nagaya - Nishio , JAPAN

This is my first time logging on. I've heard alot of good things, therefore, I'm looking forward to being a part of it. God Bless!
Darlene Duncan – Colton , CA

Well, this is my second visit today!! And, yes, I am at work -- recent to Atl from Phl -- on the rumor of all the positive things going on here -- as an IT person myself, your website, the content, the look and feel is one of the most positive I've encountered so far -- Keep up the very fine work
Jeanne Venney - Atlanta , GA

I just started checking this web site out. So far I'm liking it a lot. We need more organizations such as this one today. The idea for getting the youth more and more involved in computers is a beautiful thing. All of you are to be commended. I will be coming back to this site to see what other interesting things you're doing to help the children in the community to be inspired to do more with PC's in their everyday life. Hats Off To You!!!!
Gaynelle Fonville - Richmond , Va

This is a great program! Our school has a technology night, it will be January 11 at 7:00 pm . We will have a special technology program that is given only to a few schools across the nation. I would like to highlight your program, "PCs to the People" and give away a computer to a deserving student. How do you choose your students? Can you help me with this project? The added publicity might bring in more help for you.
Sincerely,
JoAnn Jones, Holcomb Bridge Middle School Roswell , GA

Your organization is truly an inspiration for those of our community. This revolution may not be televised ... but you are getting the word to the masses in this new medium of communication. I wish you the best.
Frank J. Williams, Sr. - Charlotte , NC

Our hero - Yes you all are. Hats off to the energy, compassion, love and most of all the willingness to surrender and serve. God will continue to bless you for being obedient. A. Houser - Lithia Springs , GA
I really enjoyed learning more about your organization. It is unique in a sense that it is using computers to bridge the gap. I hope to hear and learn more about your organization in the very near future
Constance Harvey - Marietta , GA

I heard about your website during your guest appearance on the 107.5 F.M., Sunday a.m., talk show, this morning. I had to check it out. Based upon what I found, I'm glad I did! David Thurmond - Decatur , GA
This is the first time hearing about your website. It was mentioned in the Atlanta Constitution today and I became curious. I agree with you 100% regarding our people perceptions. We must convey the message throughout

our communities/environments that being able to access and process information globally from the home will be another utility. The computer will be the vehicle. The saying, "It takes a village.....". is absolutely true. We must all offer support. ......I will be more than happy to volunteer my time and assist in any way possible. KEEP UP THE GOOD WORK!!!!!!!
Ramon Colvin - Locust Grove , GA

I am most grateful to see African Americans doing such positive things in the community, especially the cyber-community. Keep up the good work and stay positive. LaMia Saxby - Atlanta , GA

I am new viewer to your site. What caught my eye initially was your Core Values. The part about, we will not fight fire with fire, but we will fight fire with water and to build rather than destroy; to listen as intently and purposefully as we speak, etc. MY SENTIMENTS, LOUD AND CLEAR. I also believe that each one of us has a responsibility to do something. (Each 1 Teach 1) Be it volunteering or just in our own neighborhoods. Form cleanup crews, if that is what's needed. Whatever needs to be done. We don't have to wait until the government decides to throw us some crumbs before we react. We should all be focusing on the same thing and that's to ensure that when our children take our place, that they will be well equipped with the knowledge and support that they will need to be successful. I will now go back and check out the rest of your site. Thank you and continued success to you and your site.
Gustavia Clark - Paramount , CA

Hi, Mr. Kenyada, I received your website address from a friend and how bless we are today. We as African-American have the power through knowledge and I thank GOD for you sharing this knowledge. I salute you in your endeavors and may GOD bless, lead and guide you all the way. Thanks.... Rosa Martin - Indianapolis , IN

Mr. Kenyada I am so thankful for your site. My brother called me last night because of information you had that would benefit my students interested in computer technology. He found you by accident. Thank you again.
Jill Beracki - Atlanta , GA

Hotep. This is a blessing for our youth. We must educate ourselves. "Education is the passport to the future for those that prepare for it today." Malcolm X ...... Keep on striving. Ragesouljah - Oakland , CA

I reviewed your site after reading the AJC. It is truly a well-organized website. Since I teach computer desktop application classes, my initial interest was on your computer literacy article. If you ever need someone to conduct a free training class let me know.
Cardell Webb - Smyrna , GA

Richard, I would like to commend you on seeing your vision come to reality. You had a dream about this site and now many share your dream. Keep up the good work and God Bless You. Willie J. Welcome - Riverdale , GA

The senior citizens we trained were all so appreciative of the free classes...
"Thanks. You folks are angels sent to patiently help us. Please don't stop! We have information and want to share it. You are helping us to conquer our 'fears' and technical ignorance. Thanks, thanks, thanks." P.M., Decatur
"I like the slow pace of this program so we can absorb the new technique having come from years of using the print and written media. The transference to computer is more difficult for me but I was able to digest it in this program, and have been able to pull together all the bits and pieces I learned from other programs. The program is comprehensive and helped me lose my fear of using my computer. Thank you, Mr. Kenyada and your staff for your patience. in teaching us and helping us to get over the hurdle of the computer." M.H., Decatur, GA

"Thank you for giving me an opportunity to participate in the computer class for senior citizens. Thanks again for your time, your energy and your commitment. God bless you." E.K., Decatur, GA

"This is a very good and worthwhile workshop, especially for seniors who are going back into the working world." L.F., Stone Mountain, GA
"Seniors Computer Workshop for me is the best workshop to date. Instructors were knowledgeable, friendly, helpful. Every senior should have

a computer with workshops like this one to gain more knowledge about this information tool. J.C., Decatur, GA

"*The workshop is valuable and contributes to development of skills needed/required in today's culture. Further, the skills are becoming even more necessary as time passes.*" *A.B., Lithonia, GA*

"*I am now excited about computers. Before, I was afraid of them, intimidated by them, wanted no part of them. Today, I can't wait to get my own computer. It makes me think I have conquered something in my late years.*" *E.C., Lithonia, GA*

"*This class is the most wonderful class ever! The atmosphere is breathtaking. Wonderful. Wonderful.*" *G.M., Atlanta, GA*

"*The workshop was very informative and well organized. We were given some very resourceful information for future reference. The staff was well prepared and professional, very knowledgeable on the subject matter. I applaud Mr. Kenyada for his dedicated work, giving to the community. His web site is outstanding and the design is one that all African Americans should be proud of because it displays our heritage: The Red -- (Blood), Black--(people), and Green --(Land). The layout is outstanding. Very excellent workshop and I would recommend it to anyone.*" *B.M., Decatur*
"*I have thoroughly enjoyed the computer workshop. I appreciate the small class and the individualized attention..*" *E.B., Lithonia, GA*

"*I loved this course! I don't feel so afraid of playing on a computer now - AND - maybe, just maybe, I will be able to sit next to my grandchildren and not be so intimidated. Thanks.*" *M.M., Atlanta, GA*

"*This has been an extremely enjoyable and educational experience for me; a wonderful introduction to the Computer Age, which I had been avoiding for a long time. I am more informed - thanks to Mr. Kenyada and his wonderful team of volunteers. I am launched into the Computer Age. Thanks to all of you.*" *J.R., Stone Mountain, GA*

"I arrived to this class with a headache, confusion, fear (terribly afraid to touch a key!) and I can honestly leave with respect, confidence and I can now complete my own work - no more waiting for family and friends. YAHOO!! A thousand times Thank You...." N.T., Lithonia, GA

Dear Mr. Kenyada:
I recently read about the wonderful contribution that Mr. Kenyada's Neighborhood made to local students for their outstanding educational accomplishment. I commend you on your efforts of helping the youth of our community. I would also like to congratulate you on the fifth anniversary of your non-profit organization. This is a wonderful accomplishment and it shows the commitment you have to our children and their future.
Continue to be of service to our children, If I can be of assistance in your efforts, please do not hesitate to contact my office.
Sincerely,
Denise L. Majette
Member of Congress, 4th District, Georgia

Dear Mr. Kenyada:
I am encouraged by your organization's efforts and wish you success in your endeavors. Technology literacy is an important component in our efforts to provide a quality workforce for the high-tech industry. Efforts such as yours will contribute positively to our growing economy.
Sincerely,
Roy E. Barnes
Governor
State of Georgia

As it turned out, the website was an overwhelming success - both as an instrument of communication, and as a base of operations for MKN, the organization. Our community-based computer literacy initiative reached every segment of the disadvantaged neighborhoods of south DeKalb County, Georgia. In 2001, Mr. Kenyada was hired by Bellsouth Corporation to create computer training classes for families in predominately African American communities in Fulton, Clayton and DeKalb Counties. The model program reached children, adults and seniors. And by sharing our experiences, we have had an impact on similar programs around the world, advising other groups on how to go about launching their own computer literacy programs.

The so-called Digital Divide may not be totally bridged yet, but we have done our part - particularly in the early years of the struggle - to enable disadvantaged families and senior citizens along the technology superhighway. We did it all with no political or civic connections.. And it all began with just one guy standing up to accept the challenge.

ACKNOWLEDGMENTS

This book, as every plateau I've reached, is a tribute to Ajax Park in Jamaica Queens and all the people who made it what it was back in the 1960's including... *Milton Oliver, Martin & Melvin Tribble, John Bewley, Alphonso Farnell, Valerie Farnell, Gee, Buster the dog, Tito, Cooper, Tyrone Mormon, Carmon Johnston, Skipper, Big Butch, Dwight, Benjie, Al and Wayne Butler , Doug Perry and brother Kenny, Sonny Dove, Leslie "Legs" Wright, Leonard "Inch" Wright, brothers Preston, Roger, Warren and little sister Penny, Gerald Straw & brother Clyde, Roger Fleming and brother Donnie Fleming, Dianne Havens, Michelle Holder, Big Charlie Mac, Coach Sam Williams, Joey Washington, Corky Bell and brother "Pecky" Bell, George Wilson, Terry the Ice Cream Man, Roger Smith, Mary Gordon, Bunny, Joe Scott, Bill Gordon, Tom Crater, George Dye, Lee Dye, Ajax "Parkies" Park Attendants, Muscles, Davie Hill, The Ramseys - Arthur, Bobby & Arnold, Billy Moran and Lincoln Park, Milton Ray, Charles Piggot, Billy Orr, Muhammad "Raymond" A. Majid and brothers Robin LaBorde & Nicky, Big Freddie, Arthur "Big Pope" Pawpau, Mike "Little Pope" Pawpau, Joe Campbell, Clifton Jones, Beverly Mahan, Robbie Peterson, Victor Bouchet, Donny Gripper, Diane Thompson, The Favors Brothers, Ray Jacobs, Leslie "Gator" Branch, Bob Beamon, Edwina King, Mike Cambridge, Tee Hoyle, Jackie Ward, Wayne Foles, Deborah Harper, Lewis MacLeod, Cliff Patterson, Cheryl Beauford & Pumpkin, Gene & Evrod Williams, Olivia Upshur, Chick & Lee, The DeLeons, Wanda Naggles, Anita Keyes, Clyde Lewis, Popeye Stanley, Garland, Big Mike, Selley, the Other Wayne Butler, good friend and jazz artist Onaje Allan Gumbs ...and, Shimer Junior High School & P.S. 123, teachers Mr. Nathan Bright, Mrs. Burnett, Mrs. Barnett, Ms. English, Mr. Clairmont, Mr. Perlman, Mrs. Lorraine C. Harper*...and finally, to those loved ones, who stood in the background, never allowing us to quit or fail: *Pearlene & Bill Bewley, Ann & Buddy Harper, Mr. & Mrs. Ramsey, Mr. & Mrs. Holland, Mrs. Farnell, Mr. & Mrs. Jamieson, Mr. & Mrs. Straw, Clarence Culpepper, Mr. & Mrs. Butler, Alberta & Charles Russell, Eugene & Georgia Stout, James Harper, Willis Atwell... and finally, my heartfelt thanks to my good friend, Clara Delay, for editing and promoting this project.*

ABOUT THE AUTHOR

Born in Brooklyn, and raised in Jamaica, New York, Richard Kenyada served four years in the U.S. Air Force, including two tours of duty in Vietnam. He has enjoyed a 40-year career in the engineering profession. In addition, he is most proud of the community work he has successfully completed in an effort to promote computer literacy.

In 2004, Richard published his first book, "Essays & Open Wounds While Waiting for The APOLOGY," a collection of issues and answers central to the black experience. The book's central work, "The APOLOGY," was adapted as the finale to the stage production "The MAAFA Suite," which toured the country under the direction of the St. Paul Community Baptist Church based in Brooklyn, NY. Kenyada lives in a suburb of Atlanta with his wife, Patricia.

www.ingramcontent.com/pod-product-compliance
Lightning Source LLC
Chambersburg PA
CBHW020914290526
45784CB00002BA/547